**The
Headless Hammerhead
Guide to Entrepreneurship**
and Other Advice for Business

The Headless Hammerhead Guide to Entrepreneurship
and Other Advice for Business

By Giovanni V. Crisan

Phase II Publishing ☺ Ft. Lauderdale, FL
THIS IS A SAVING PHASE BOOK PUBLISHED BY PHASE II PUBLISHING

The opinions, views, and ideas contained in this book are strictly those of the author and do not reflect those of Phase II Publishing, its subsidiaries, or its business partners. Phase II Publishing accepts no liability for any consequences of actions taken on the basis of the information provided herein.

Text copyright © 2018, 2016, 2014 by Giovanni V. Crisan
Cover photograph © 2012, 2018 by Giovanni V. Crisan
Author Photograph © 2018 by Giovanni V. Crisan

All rights reserved.
No part of this book may be used or reproduced in any manner whatsoever without written permission except in the case of brief quotations embodied in critical articles and reviews.
Published in the United States by Phase II Publishing, Ft. Lauderdale.

Saving Phase and the Headless Hammerhead and Phase II logos are trademarks of Phase II Publishing.

Designed and edited by Giovanni V. Crisan

Crisan, Giovanni V.
The Headless Hammerhead Guide to Entrepreneurship and Other Advice for Business / by Giovanni V. Crisan

SUMMARY:
Most new businesses fail within the first two years of operation - don't be one of them! Prepare yourself with a clear, concise, step-by-step guide to starting and running your business - from registering with the government to knowing your numbers, creating competitive advantages, branding, and tips for your daily operation. This book is easy to read and navigate, and includes summary pages at the end of each section to provide at-a-glance access to key points from the chapters you've already read.

The Headless Hammerhead Guide to Entrepreneurship and Other Advice for Business will provide you with tons of invaluable information in one place without pretense or complicated explanations. Get your business up and running the right way - the Headless Hammerhead way!

ISBN: 9781729259030

Printed in the United States of America

New Phase II Publishing trade paperback edition December 2018

For my brother Vase;
the only Headless Hammerhead I know
who has his head on straight.

Introduction

"I lost my head so you wouldn't have to."
                                    -Me

It was late 2000 and I was doing very well at my job with Airborne Express. I had just received a promotion, and I decided I wanted to explore the possibility of starting a business. So, I started reading about planning for business and about accounting.

I decided to start a business and initially set my sights on a sushi restaurant. At the time, sushi was the food trend *du jour*, yet nobody offered sushi delivery in my area (a very densely populated Yuppie area in Miami called Doral), and after researching the industry I found sushi delivery to be almost nonexistent anywhere in the US. However, the statistics on restaurant start-ups are very dismal, so my attention turned to finding a suitable, sustainable, and scalable business I could open with my limited experience; a friend recommended I open a tanning salon.

Although I had never tanned in a tanning booth before in my life (and although I lived in South Florida and was within minutes of the beach, I rarely took the time to go), I began to research the industry. I learned a lot about tanning salons and the industry in general, customer trends based on local weather, demographics, the law and regulations, and of course, the scientific data that either supports or debunks claims about the dangers of indoor tanning.

During my research, I also began working on a business plan – in the end, the business plan was more than 65 pages long, and included everything from worst-case to (the often-missed) best-case scenario, marketing, sales strategies, dealing with picketers who oppose indoor tanning salons, and many other issues in between.

The tanning salon opened in 2002 and is still (October 2018) operating. The company made a profit its first year, and enjoyed a steady revenue flow the entire time I owned it. In 2006, I proposed to my partner (who was ironically my fiancée at the time, so pardon the pun) that we expand as a franchise and go public. Part of my plan was to sell all my shares within five years and move on to another venture.

But, my relationship with my partner suddenly ended shortly after that, and rather than begin what could prove to be decades-long litigation, I sold all my shares of the business for $10. This is not a decision I regret; rather, what I regret is going into business with her in the first place.

To this day, she continues to run the one salon, making a decent living but complacent with stagnant or nonexistent growth. I handled her accounting for a few years after I gave up my shares in the company, and I realized that her unwillingness to give up equity in her business had put her in a place that made the company a job for her rather than an investment.

I've since opened several companies and helped many other companies through consulting, and I've found many similarities between my ex's situation and that of struggling small business owners. I've also seen TV shows like *The Profit*, *Shark Tank*, *Bar Rescue*, *Restaurant Impossible* and others, and find some of the same recurring themes among other business owners as well.

There are many guides out there on starting a business or running a successful small business, but few, if any, offer a comprehensive, step-by-step process, backed by free, live consulting like I offer through my website, www.HeadlessHammerhead.com. While reading through this book please keep in mind that successful companies, like successful countries, are not run by a single person.

Surround yourself with the best talent and always keep an open mind; and be willing to take a risk. Good luck on your journey. Like Plato said, "The beginning is the most important part of the work."

I hope you get something out of this text, and I hope your success helps you stand out in a sea of entrepreneurial sharks!

-*Giovanni V. Crisan*

Contents

1. Your Joy – Making Money?..................... 7
2. Avoiding Business Abortion – Yikes!....... 27
3. Sell Hair to a Werewolf......................... 39
4. Trust the Experts................................. 53
5. The Devil You Know.............................. 67
6. Value Meals vs. Company Values.......... 77
7. Have a Vision... 87
8. ...and a Mission.................................... 97
9. Go on the Journey................................ 107
10. Fostering Your Ideas........................... 119
11. What Type of Company is This?........... 127
12. Play by the Numbers........................... 137
13. Here's the Plan................................... 155
14. Legalease... 169
15. Protect Your Brand.............................. 185
16. Leverage Your Advantage.................... 199
17. Communication................................... 213
18. Your Core Business.............................. 221
19. Daily Operation................................... 231
20. Networking... 253
21. Opinions and Business......................... 269
22. Criticism and Business......................... 277
23. Being a Champion................................ 287
24. The Folly of Being a Low-Cost Provider 301
25. Your Weaknesses................................. 307
26. Kids, Pets, and Your Company.............. 315
27. Be Charitable...................................... 325
28. Diversify and Defy............................... 333
29. Looking Ahead..................................... 341
30. When Failure is Your Only Option......... 349

Your Joy - Making Money?

*"It's important to love the product, but it's **really** important to love the business."*
–Robert Herjavec

Welcome, Entrepreneur!

My idea for this text is to keep the conversation informal; I didn't want to create a preachy, formal text that is self-serving. Rather, I wanted to create a platform where any entrepreneur, whether it be a high school student or a career investor, could read a random page and think to him/herself, "oh yeah, I could do that!"

In this spirit, I've designed a text that's more like a blog, where each chapter after "Avoiding Business Abortion – Yikes!" (Chapter 2) can be taken out of its context and still be easily understood. That said, please feel free to jump around – don't limit yourself to the linear way of reading a book, but rather focus on those topics you feel you need to address first. This way you can go back and read them again after you've tackled the entire thing - not just for repetition's sake, but to drill the points home.

I will ask, however, that you not pick-and-choose what to read and what not to read. If you do that, you may miss an important facet of running a business, and it can lead you to more obstacles than you already have to face as an entrepreneur.

So, this chapter explores the conundrum many of us face when starting a business: figuring out our true motivation for starting that business and figuring out if what we want is to have a job or to be a true entrepreneur. There is *absolutely* a difference, and many entrepreneurs, especially those who run family-owned businesses or who have a passion or hobby they want to turn into a career, fall into the trap of opening a business that in reality becomes their nine-to-five and nothing more.

I'm not going to waste your time here – let's get right into it: why did you decide to start a business? Seriously think about this and write down your answers. Did you really like balloons and thought opening a party store would have you close to balloons all day while paying you a salary? Did you think balloon technology would rival the next iPhone and decide to go into it as an investment for your future? Are balloons really hot right now and you thought you'd capitalize on the trends? Do you have 19 kids and counting and think they'd really like to have balloons around the house all the time?

If you're being honest with yourself, you should have a **single-main motivator** or driver that led you to this decision of becoming an entrepreneur. Now, if your primary motivation is not about making money for your present or future, then you really need to have a conversation with yourself (again?) about your plans for your future and about calculated risks.

Do not allow your own biases, likes, obsessions, etc. cloud your judgment – believe me when I tell you that every southerner thinks theirs is the best barbecue sauce in the world. Trust me when I tell you that everyone thinks they will have a multi-million dollar barbershop because they do the best fades. And don't doubt the fact that everyone thinks they're gonna be the next Dr. Dre when they start their own record label because they have the best local rappers or songwriters.

If this offends you, it's time for a reality check. Put yourself in the shoes of your target customer. If you're walking down the street and Blake Shelton asks you to please take a free copy of his new cd, you'd likely take it – whether it's because you're a fan or you think you can sell it to someone who is. Now, if a no-name nobody hands you a free copy of their new country cd, how likely are you to listen to it more than once? How likely are you to listen to it at all? We'll talk about marketing and valuing your product later, but think about what your answer to these questions would be if you had actually paid for the music.

You can apply this to any business you're thinking of starting. Free haircut? Sure. But I like my regular barber, so you've just wasted your time trying to get me to switch. Free sample of your secret sauce? Thanks! But with free samples and millions of food companies pushing their products, odds are that that's the last time I taste it.

We delve deeper into this in our chapter about "The Folly of Being the Low-Cost Provider" and discuss competitive advantage in "Leverage Your Advantage" but for now, think about your motivations and ask strangers – not friends and family, because they'll lie to you to avoid hurting your feelings – to tell you what they think of your idea. Have an open mind, and if they say you're crazier than a dog chasing its own tail, but you still think you're right, then your persistence is admirable but you need to realize that you'll need more than a couple of muskets and batons to join the March of the Light Brigade.

*   *   *

Going into business is a major life decision, which most entrepreneurs find easy to make; they follow their passion and open a business related to that passion. However, many people start a business for the wrong reasons.

Think of how many people believe they can sing or play a sport - and then think of how many actually make it in those industries. Go to almost any high school and you'll find dozens, if not hundreds, of would-be professional athletes and musicians *in each one*.

I, myself, have a passion. Well, maybe I'm starting a little too far along in the story here - let's roll back the clock a little bit.

I was watching TV the other day and I caught the end of a show about some investors looking to find the next big product or company; it's called *Shark Tank*. The premise involves amateur entrepreneurs trying to achieve the American Dream by getting one of these investors to agree to go in on their ideas with a sizable investment that would allow that entrepreneur to scale their business's operation or maybe just get their ideas realized altogether.

During this particular episode, one of the investors was intrigued by the idea a couple of women entrepreneurs had that would do something great for some disadvantaged people in Africa - all while providing a unique, high-quality product at a reasonable price for the consumer. This investor, however moved he may have been by the story these two women told, responded with something that rang so true I wish I could repeat it to every single entrepreneur I meet without coming off as rude or preachy.

What did he say? It was something in the vein of, "this is great and it warms my heart, but HOW WILL IT *MAKE ME MONEY*?"

Now, before you whip out your list of expletives and email them to me, let me explain why I think this is a crucial question to ask yourself if you are a serious entrepreneur.

I know most of us have many things we're passionate about. Some of these things run so deep in our veins that we feel compelled to make a business out of it. Generally, there's nothing wrong with that. If you like to get creative with people's hair or makeup, you may want to open a beauty salon or start a cosmetology business. When I was a kid I met a guy so passionate about baseball cards and comic books that he opened a local "Cards and Comics" store (which is where I met him). I loved going there because this guy knew his stuff; he knew everything that was going on in the various series of comics, and he knew which baseball cards would be the next best ones to save in a hard acrylic display holder.

I remember once wanting to buy some cards off of him, and he was selling them for more than the cards were currently worth because he said Darryl Strawberry and a few others were going to be *huge*.

Here's the problem with this guy's business, though: he was **too** passionate about the <u>comics and cards</u> (the product) and not passionate enough about <u>making money</u> (the business). There was no question that this guy knew his stuff - he knew the product inside and out - but he didn't know his **business** inside and out. The sad reality is that the best he could ever hope for, like the cosmetician or hairstylist, is to make a *living*, rather than make serious money. And if that's what makes you happiest, then that's almost all you'll ever need. Maybe the people on that show I mentioned could start a nonprofit to help these ladies in Africa and they could feel fulfilled for the rest of their lives. But... to make it big, this "Cards and Comics" guy - I think his name was Rob - needed to focus more on *growing his business*. He could have sold that card that cost him maybe ten cents and made a huge profit selling it for $20 or even $50, but his passion for the sport prevented him from making money – and he priced the card so that it *wouldn't* sell.

I found out much later in life that eventually Rob closed shop in the early 2000's, which serves as proof of his biggest mistake. The key here is that even a small business needs to plan for at least *some* growth. Even if to offset any unforseeables like a lawsuit, government regulation, increased taxes, cost of living, or whatever.

But Rob's passion for baseball cards and comic books *made him blind to shortcomings* in his business. I'm willing to bet that, on a bad month, he convinced himself that the next big "crossover event" in a popular comic book would dig him out of a hole. Or perhaps he thought the next Mickey Mantle would have a special limited edition version of the card that would bring him a big payoff and keep him in the black.

His passion for the sport and the comics, however, blinded him to the possibility of Darryl Strawberry having substance abuse issues, or of Jose Canseco writing a bestselling book naming several top players as anabolic steroid users - which, of course, made many of these players lose all credibility as great athletes. Thus, cards that could have been worth thousands today are worth $150 or less. Now, that may sound like a pretty good return on a card that only cost a few cents, but we can't ignore the *time value of money*, nor the harsh reality of inflation over this period of time.

The big takeaway here is that if you have a passion that drives you to open a business, you first need to have an honest, soul-searching introspection to determine if your business idea is one that can truly make you a millionaire or if your passion for the product or service would overtake your passion for making money. If it's the latter, you may be dooming yourself to becoming part of that infamous "80% of businesses fail" statistic - and nobody wants that.

This doesn't mean that your daily goal is to get the green. What it means is that your focus, your ultimate goal, is to grow the business to where it can not only sustain you and your family, but other employees and their families as well. You don't just want to "make a living", do you?

I've seen many articles online, other books, etc. that'll tell you to focus on "making a difference" or "creating change". Keep in mind that you can't get very far doing those things if you don't have any money; if those are your goals - your passions - you should start a nonprofit organization instead. This way you could do some good while still making a living.

Remember the warning you get when you set foot on an airplane – if there's an emergency, save yourself first;

then help others. In business, you must first make a profit, hire employees, and then make a difference.

Am I being too harsh here? Probably. And what about all those people who, like "Papa" John Schnatter, had a passion and a vision to create a company that was better than some of the giants in play at the time? What about companies like Starbucks, Ben and Jerry's, or some of the more successful upstarts like Chewy.com?

Don't be dissuaded by the people who tell you large corporations are evil. All of the companies I've listed above have and have had investors whose sole motivation was for these companies to succeed so that they can grow and provide hefty returns. But most large corporations are very charitable (there is a chapter on this later), as are many wealthy people. But again, if you feel guilty about making money or having money be as much of a motivator as your cause or passion, start a nonprofit 501(c)3. I have more information on that on page 522 of this book.

* * *

If you've stuck around so far in this chapter, I'd be willing to wager that you're motivated to actually go beyond simply "surviving" in your chosen industry and want to actually thrive. Congratulations!

So now you probably think that I'm the next Gordon Gekko, right? Well, although my main goal is to get you to want and get money, greed is not good. Greed, just like an obsession with Barbie dolls that motivates you to open a toy shop, can lead to complete business failure. If this seems like I'm contradicting myself, please read on for an explanation.

The reason I imply at the beginning of this chapter that money should be your primary motivator is to try and get you out of the mentality that a passion is enough to make you successful. I am firmly aware that being a fan of watches can lead me to open a very lucrative watch business. However, an entrepreneur can't allow herself to be blinded by emotional attachments to her business. I'll use my own story as an example.

Against most of my family and friends' warnings, I opened a tanning salon in the Sunshine State, of all places. And, contrary to the expectations of my family and friends, it was successful. It still is. But, the person who owns it now has had it for about ten years, and her revenue has not changed. As inflation grows, that means she's actually losing money every year.

What I would have done differently had I kept the tanning salon is stick to my business plan. I placed a **limit order** on my own business, so that if it grew to a certain level in terms of sales, I was going to make it a franchise, and I would have sought out investors through sales of stock in the company so that I could continue to grow the company into a nationwide franchise corporation. Then I would have sold my shares.

Don't fall into the trap of seeing your company as your "baby", because you will be reluctant to give up any equity in the future. The fact that the tanning salon made money through the Great Recession – a time when most people cut luxuries like tanning out of their budgets and many major companies failed – was a great indicator of the potential of the company. But that potential was never fully realized.

Don't let this happen to you. If you have a child, would you want that child to remain at home all day playing for the rest of his life, or would you want to see him become the next Dr. Oz?

If you have a hammer and hold it in your hand all the time and walk around until you see a nail to bang on, then you've become what some call the "tool of the tool". But if you work on making your house the best it can be every day and during one of those days you notice a nail that needs to be hammered in – and only then do you reach for the hammer – now *you own the tool*.

If you're serious about running a successful business, then get serious about it. ***Treat it like a business, an investment, not like a family member***.

But, a word of warning. An example used by entrepreneurship classes as a cautionary case study is that of Wally Amos, known for his "Famous Amos" brand of cookies. Wally is a very nice guy who was very proud of his cookie recipe, because all his family and friends loved it. They eventually talked him into making a business out of it.

Wally, however, didn't care much about the business end of the company – he just wanted to make and sell cookies. So, he introduced some investors and started his brand. After a few years of success, scaling the business became quite costly, so he raised more capital in exchange for equity, and he scaled the business.

We'll delve deeper into this when we discuss numbers later in this book, but not knowing his numbers and failing to utilize creative methods to grow the business doomed Amos into thinning out his own shares of the company. Eventually, he owned almost nothing, and even lost his brand, *Famous Amos,* and rights to his name as a result.

The key here is to know where you want your company to go and, more importantly, how you plan on getting there. Work closer to that goal every day, and don't get complacent. If you stick to a plan, you will be successful.

On the flip side, you don't want to sell airplane parts if you know nothing about airplanes. This could be a gigantic mistake, because it can cause you to make terrible decisions for your business and it can cost you as well during negotiations.

In my own example, I knew nothing about indoor tanning when I decided to start a tanning business in South Florida. However, before opening my doors - before putting any money into the business - I researched the industry for over a year, and I learned everything there was to know about tanning, skin cancer, tanning beds, tanning lotions, melanin, vitamin D synthesis, etc.

By the time I opened my doors, nobody could walk into my place and debate me about indoor tanning without getting owned. So, when you hear people say that you must be passionate about your product, what they *really mean* is that you need to understand who your customer is – what motivates them, what attracts them to your product or service, what are the demographics. In other words, what makes *your customer* passionate about your product or service.

I opened a tanning salon – selling sunshine in the Sunshine State – and succeeded against all odds because I knew the business and I knew the product and I knew the customer. Would I have been as successful if I had opened the tanning salon in a South Florida neighborhood where most residents are black? My doors would be closed before I even opened them.

One of the banks to whom I presented my business plan while looking for initial capital asked us if she could keep a copy of my business plan. I agreed, and shortly thereafter the loan officer's cousin opened a tanning salon in Hialeah, Florida at one of the locations we had scouted - just two months before *we* opened *our* doors. It was obvious to me the loan officer thought all the hard work was done, and had her cousin simply open his salon using my business plan. Easy money, right?

I had decided against that location after polling the local community for three weeks; turns out the people of Hialeah felt that they weren't gonna pay for tanning if they could tan for free at the beach or in their back yards using baby oil. That means they wouldn't have even bought one of the most profitable products tanning salons offer: the tanning lotions.

My competitor lasted three months before having to close his doors. My tanning salon, almost 20 years later, is still operating successfully even though I no longer own it.

When I had gone to this guy's location to do competitive research I asked questions about tanning and lotions, and neither he nor his wife had a clue what the different lotions' benefits were or what the difference between an upright (standing) versus a flat (lay-down) tanning booth was. It was obvious he had gone into it simply to make money, but he hadn't taken the time to learn about his product or customer.

Take the time to learn your whole business - both the product and the business end - and you will be able to jump over most of the hurdles many entrepreneurs seem to constantly trip over.

- Think about why you want to open a business
    - Hobby?
    - Charity?
    - Job?
    - Money?
    - Fame?
    - Legacy?

- Going into business is like making an Investment:
    - Expect growth
    - Expect returns
    - Don't expect the business to be yours forever
    - Know your customers (who is buying this product/service? Why?)
    - Know your product or service – inside and out
    - Use your product or service to live the customer experience

Avoiding Business Abortion – Yikes!

*"O God! Can I not grasp
Them with a tighter clasp?"*
        -Edgar Allan Poe, A Dream Within a Dream

This topic is probably one of the more controversial ones in this book. However, it should help lead you to help your business reach its ultimate growth potential. This chapter delves deeper into why loving your business too much can lead to disaster.

I mentioned in "Your Joy – Making Money?" (Chapter 1) that starting a business is a lot like having a baby; you create it, you name it, you hold its hand and guide it to success. Yet unlike with a child, many business owners forget that at some point they need to let the bird leave the nest. Businesses, if successful, will take a life of their own; and you, as an entrepreneur and "business parent" need to learn to allow it to succeed, rather than stunt its growth because of your own selfishness.

In keeping with the theme from last chapter, I wanted to bring to light the idea that your business is "your baby" and then turn it on its head. This chapter may be more controversial than that one simply because it will probably feel like I am attacking your family; particularly, I am about to attack your baby and it's not gonna feel good. So if you're sensitive about these things, please turn to page 522 for some relaxation techniques before you try to tackle this monster.

Being an entrepreneur myself, I know the pride that comes with starting your business or creating your product: seeing your logo on a sign or billboard, seeing reviews on social media, reading your awesome title on a business card out loud. Owner. CEO. President. It's as good a feeling as having your kid become the next President of the United States.

But I am about to take that business card and rip it into hundreds of little pieces right in front of your face. Well, not me, but I'm gonna ask *you* to do it. Go ahead, try it: if you have one, rip one of your business cards to shreds.

How did that feel? I bet it was a devastating feeling. Having everything you've worked hard for, taking your ideas – some that probably took months or years to develop – and throwing them away. I'll be the bearer of the news that as an entrepreneur you're gonna need to get used to this feeling, but not always for negative reasons. Let me explain.

My first business was a tanning salon. Yes, I actually sold sunshine in the Sunshine State. I planned for over a year, researching the industry, trends, viability in my market, competition, location, and much, much more. I wrote a 65-plus page business plan, and I was very proud of that. Even the bank loan specialists were impressed with the plan and many asked for copies to keep, all after denying me a loan; but there are two important points here.

First, I opened the business with my fiancée at the time (again, there's another chapter dedicated to starting a business with friends and family – see *Chapter 5: The Devil You Know*). My second problem was actually related to the first: my fiancée felt all those giddy things

I mentioned in the POTUS paragraph above, and she wanted to avoid ever feeling like her child had been taken away from her.

We had lotions made and branded with our trademarked logo. We had a really cool website that I designed and updated weekly with promotions and information. We had a customer base that really wanted to support us through what later became known as "The Great Recession".

When the business grew to a point where I felt it was time to expand (i.e., a second location, franchising the brand, etc.) she did not want **anyone else** to have a controlling interest in the company. Not even 5%. And to avoid a lengthy discussion or fight, I went along with her wishes.

Then, just over a year later, our relationship came to an end. We had a brief discussion about the business, and I decided to sell her my share of it for $10. Most of my family and friends believe that was a mistake. But, an entrepreneur needs to be able to see when a decision or product or service or spokesperson is going to create a hemorrhage that could prove to be the company's own extinction asteroid. I had cut my losses and moved on; I knew I could open another tanning salon if I wanted to, and maybe even buy her out eventually - but I never really cared for the tanning business. In fact, when I started to research the industry, I had not ever tanned in an indoor tanning salon and I rarely went to the beach. To me, the tanning salon was simply an investment.

Had I tried to fight for a share of that business, though, I'd probably still be fighting for it ten years later, and only the lawyers would be making any money off of it. Thing is, I had planned for this (and many other crazy scenarios) in my business plan. I'd even planned for an often-missed "best case scenario" (in which the business grows too quickly to be sustainable). The tanning salon is still afloat, but it's not making my ex-fiancée a millionaire by any means.

So, the lesson here is to learn to kill that baby. If your bar is losing money every month, but you feel bad for your employees, or you want to fight until the bitter end, your baby will not be the only thing that dies; you and your family and any investors you have will go down with that ship quicker than Edward J. Smith.

Of course, you may go through some grief after such a loss. Nobody said it would be easy. Watch the movie 127 hours so you can see first-hand (pun intended!) just how difficult this decision can be. In the end, though, cutting off a dead limb can save your life. Your employees will find other work; don't put more importance on yourself than there should be. You can open another business; this is not your only chance at the American Dream, and all is not lost if you cut your losses early enough (see *Chapter 30: When Failure is Your Only Option*).

Now, losing your company is not always the result of something awful; it can be that an investor has offered you a ton of money for an interest in the company, they've offered to buy you out outright, or you are at the crossroads where your future growth or scalability depends on selling equity in your company. You may fear that another owner will want to change your logo or alter the name of your company, or change its processes, its culture, or change its vision drastically.

If you fear any of these, think of Facebook; before Mark Zuckerberg met with Sean Parker, his website was known as "The Facebook" and only allowed people to join if they had a college or university email address. The changes that Zuckerberg agreed to make changed Facebook and propelled it into becoming the giant it is today.

If you have children, ask yourself if you would want to prevent that child from achieving her full potential. If you don't have children, this could be an exercise in allowing a future child to leave the nest, or even as an exercise in being possessive in relationships. Remember that corporations are viewed by the government as separate entities from their owners; they have their own unique identifiers (Tax ID's or EIN's) that act like social security numbers. They pay taxes and have legal liabilities and responsibilities just like individual people. Basically, incorporating creates a new entity, so it will no longer be completely yours, since even in the eyes of the law it is now a separate entity.

This means that *you'll* need to treat your company in this way, too – even if you haven't incorporated or don't plan to do so, start getting used to it, because you never know what the law might say about sole proprietorships in the future. Avoid becoming a tyrannical dictator or authoritarian parent and serve your purpose instead as a guide who is there to groom this entity into becoming the next greatest thing. Again, this won't be easy.

To prepare yourself for such a traumatic possibility, I recommend buying a graphics tablet like the Buddha, Adesso, or Crayola, then write or draw something amazing every day or every week and wipe it clean (or let it clear itself). This will help you learn the Zen art of letting go and can help you in your business decision-making. You can even get a dry-erase board at the dollar store and do this on a budget.

Another great technique is to give away a precious possession. Think about losing your smart device, laptop, etc; maybe give away a favorite shirt or shoes; or try selling one of your favorite watches or purses. The idea here is to **learn to let go**.

Then, if you get a sweetheart deal from a "White Knight" investor like those on TV, weigh the options **objectively** and then **do it**. It's usually for the best. *But!* don't just give away all your equity. Equity is valuable, so treat it that way. Read on.

*   *   *

So where is the line between giving up too much equity or being so hard-nosed that it prevents your company from advancing? The answer is not so simple, but there are many excellent strategies that can help guide you in this.

First, the amount of equity you are willing to give up in exchange for investment capital should be fair and consistent with the true current value of your company (***never*** base it on the future value – see the "Cards and Comics" example in Chapter 1).

You should try to get the best deal while giving up the least amount of equity, of course, but be willing to negotiate – don't shoot down every offer because it doesn't match your target 100%. So, if your limit is 5% and the investor's offer is 6% you may want to take a long, hard look at the possibilities and what the 1% could mean. If with the investment your company can grow by $1m, then yes, you may have just given up $10K in the short-run, but if you had not taken the deal you may be at $0. What's $10K when you just made $940K?

On the same token, if your company is already targeting close to $1m and the investment will only help increase your revenue by $50K, then that 1% is actually costing you too much. Check out the chapter on numbers for more details and examples on this concept.

The second technique you can use to help you determine whether an investment transaction is sound or not is to plan for it – yes, have a plan for your business, not just time-wise (year 1, year 2, etc.) but also growth-wise ($100K, $500K, $1m). Just like with a child, have a plan of what you'd like to achieve at each of these benchmarks. Do you want to have two locations open by the third year of operation? It would have to depend on revenue, so what is the revenue threshold? How much money would you like to have in reserves for this venture? How much do you expect to make or lose from this venture, and how would the equity you give up to an investor affect this? How much of an impact would and investment have on this venture?

One final thought: remember Famous Amos and do not get overzealous with investors in the beginning. That is, don't give up more than 40% of your equity in the first few years of your business – keep control until your business is ready to grow on its own. You'll need equity as leverage for future expansion; trust me, once it's gone, it's gone.

- Be willing to give up your business
    - Be prepared to part with your business
    - Learn the Zen art of letting go
    - Give up something you care about – can you handle it?
    - Be willing to cut off a dead limb if it's holding you back
    - Be willing to make changes other professionals recommend: business name, process, logo, etc.

- Have a plan for dealing with investors
    - Be fair with your business valuation – don't value it on what it will be worth in the future
    - Some growth is better than no growth
    - Listen to investor input
    - Plan for benchmarks
        - Time benchmarks
        - Financial benchmarks
    - Don't give up more than 40% of your business in the first few years. You'll need equity for leverage in the future

Sell Hair to a Werewolf

"[Stories] are very engaging... people go into... story mode, [and] we get out of judgment."
                    -Eben Pagan

This chapter is a little bit different than the prior ones. This one is going to be more like a "listicle," and will contain loads of information in a rather compact package. Read on!

You may have found yourself entering the sock store to get some socks to go with your new pair of slacks or way-cool pantsuit, only to be swiftly approached by an employee asking you if you need assistance. Most people in the modern era immediately, almost reflexively, respond with, "No, I'm just looking."

Getting through that wall when you're a salesperson is one of the most difficult things to master and is the main thing that keeps salespeople in the "middle-class" range of salaries.

Entrepreneurs are salespeople more than anything else – they are constantly trying to get their product, service, or idea into the hands of the consumer or investor, but many don't know how to actually do this. The following tips are some that you can start using immediately to increase your sales conversion rates.

But before I delve into the coveted list, I want to tell you a story. There was this little girl who was born with a very unusual condition: she was a type of albino that was practically allergic to the sun. This was a horrible condition for her, because she could never see the light of day, watch a sunset, or leave the house because it was a risk to her very existence. Can you imagine? Being locked up in a room all day, every day, without even being able to look outside your window!

The curious thing about this particular condition, though, is that the poor girl didn't just have a danger of meeting her demise if she stepped out into the sun; there were concerns about her going through puberty, because the female body requires so many nutrients, especially calcium, to properly develop. The problem with calcium is that it can't be absorbed in the body without vitamin D (it's vitamin D soluble). For most people, the body synthesizes vitamin D naturally with regular exposure to the sun, so most people don't need additional supplementation. Because of her condition, this girl *did* need those supplements.

But there was another problem. Vitamin D is fat soluble. This means that this little girl had to consume very fatty foods just to be able to get the vitamin D and, eventually, the calcium her body needed. And she was at an age where even if she wasn't able to leave the house, body image is everything. But being stuck in the house meant she watched a lot of TV and had very few human interactions, so her idea of what her body should look like was completely fabricated by mass media marketing – more so than most other teenage girls today. She didn't want to get fat, and she couldn't really exercise properly to burn off all the fat she needed to consume.

What a conundrum!

Luckily, most of us don't have this issue. Scientists say that it's worse for a person to never get any sun at all than to get too much sun. Of course, you don't want to get too much because of the increased chances of skin cancer if you burn; so the trick is to gradually build and maintain a decent tan, just like you would maintain proper body weight by exercising regularly and eating right without overdoing it. The fact is you can't build a tan in one day (unless you spray tan), just like you can't get in shape by going to the gym only once.

The above story is the secret to how I sold sunshine (indoor tanning) in the Sunshine State – and I never lied to anybody. I was also a responsible tanning salon owner in that I never allowed anyone to over-tan. I researched skin types and what proper exposure times would be. Sometimes that meant the person could only tan for 1-2 minutes, which is not what people are used to, but it really helped build credibility and trust with clients. I even had celebrities tan at my place.

So how can you sell bags of sand at a beach? Here are the top 7 things to *always* keep in mind when trying to sell:

1. **Don't <u>ever</u> try to sell anything**. The Japanese have a thing called *uwe*, which means "trying not to try". The single-worst thing you can do when attempting to sell something is to try and sell it to the person. Think of when you enter a department store and the sales associate approaches you. Most people's reflex response is, "I'm just browsing."

   Your product or service should sell itself, and you should be simply there as a guide – helping answer questions and guiding the decision-making process. How can you sell without selling? Simply have conversations with your clients. Talk to them learn who they are and what their interests are. Learn about their families. This will help take down the wall that is automatically raised when a salesperson approaches a customer. And highlight the benefits and how these will help the customer. Avoid talking about the features.

2. ***Tell it as a story***. The quote from Eben Pagan at the top of this chapter says it exactly like it is; if you start with a story it's easy to move in for the kill. Like my story of the little girl with the extreme form of photosensitivity, stories help people get their guard down so you can insert your pitch without the buyer ever noticing. Did you spot the pitch in my story above? Probably not. But I can guarantee that nine out of ten people, when told tanning is bad for you, would probably repeat this story as a rebuttal, thus making your sale easier the next time.

There was a lady at a department store one time who overheard a conversation I was having with my brother as we tried to decide whether to buy an LCD or LED TV. Although she butted into our conversation uninvited, we didn't mind it because she opened with this: "Oh, my God. My husband had friends over for the Big Game last year and they were having the usual: chips, pizza, and beer. When his team scored, one of his friends jumped up to do a dance, and tripped, knocking our LCD TV off the wall. The screen cracked and looked like there'd been an oil spill inside half of it, and it couldn't be fixed – that's the liquid crystal. Definitely get LED, because that won't happen with an LED."

Turns out this lady was the sales rep at the store. We had no idea until we thanked her for the vital info and she introduced herself. Had she walked up and asked if we needed help, we probably would have told her we were just browsing. Instead, she explained the difference between two similar products, made a recommendation, and got two very grateful, loyal customers who bought a tv and returned a month later to buy a laptop from her.

3. ***Simplicity is your friend.*** Don't overwhelm your client with too much unnecessary information. In the photosensitive girl story above, I gave plenty of scientific fact without overwhelming the listener. Notice that I didn't describe the different machines and which was better than the other, etc. That information can be given once the customer asks, but you are the expert based on your conversation and assessment of the client's wants and needs. This leads to the next point:

4. ***Don't give the customer too many options.*** Have a conversation. Ask about the kids. Ask about the customer's likes and dislikes. Then ask what her goals are for that bachelorette party. You can decide which two or three options you'll give the client and say something like, "Based on what you've told me, I would recommend either the life-size Spider Man statue or the Batman costume."

5. ***Know your audience and your product.***
   Although you may be an expert botanist, if an old man walks into your flower shop looking for a beautiful bouquet for his wife on their 60th anniversary, find two options and explain why you presented them. "This bouquet is nice and bright, to celebrate such a joyous occasion" or "this bouquet has five shades of blue because you said that's Ethel's favorite color (you said even her hair is blue!)."

   Don't tell this guy the names of all the flowers in that bouquet and the difference between a Sunflower and a Black-eyed Susan because it'll be overwhelming, and he would likely not remember or even care.

   Now, if the guy says he's worked on gardens all his life or has a green thumb, maybe mentioning these details would help build rapport with him. You may even be able to tell him about your "flower of the month" club and get an upsell in this way. But remember that people are all different, so just because it interests you, it may not necessarily interest them. Show passion, not obsession.

It's extremely important, however, to know your product. Nothing takes my confidence down to zero when buying from someone than when I ask a question and the person either makes up the answer or doesn't know. Which leads us to:

6. ***Don't ever lie***. I often go shopping with a pretty good idea of what I'm going to buy, and I usually research the product extensively before heading out with money in hand.

   At the store, I usually ask the salesperson a question that I already know the answer to just to see if he knows what he's talking about. If he doesn't know some things, it's ok, as long as he's honest about it and offers to find out; if he knows nothing, I go somewhere else; and if he outright lies, I publicly call him out on his bull$#!+ and then I leave. There is no reason to lie to your customers or investors – they will eventually find out that you're lying, and it's much more difficult to come back from that than to take some time to find the answer for them.

Remember that nowadays people have tons of information at their fingertips, and it's not difficult for anyone to get the truth in a matter of seconds.

7. *Assume the sale.* There's a comedy prank show called *Impractical Jokers* in which one of the hosts was challenged by his friends to rub sun block on an unsuspecting beachgoer. The host, named Murr, was initially worried about how he would pull that off, so when the challengers gave him the green light he simply went in behind the man and said, "they say the moon landing was fake," as he rubbed sunblock on the guy's body and forehead, and later even ordered daiquiris with the guy. Hilarity aside, the

confidence of the approach made the whole thing possible.

Remember, though, assuming the sale (and the old "ABC – Always Be Closing") doesn't contradict point #1. What it means is that you've built such good rapport during your interaction and through you Shakespearean-style storytelling that it wouldn't be a question whether the bachelorettes are going to buy something at your novelty store or not – it's a question of Batman versus Spider Man, or maybe you've told them the story so well that it's, without question, going to be a team-up!

When selling, just like when you're pitching investors, clients, potential distributors, or whatever, remember that if you have an offer on the table the sale is done - close it. Don't try to keep selling, because you'll just talk yourself out of a deal. Simply congratulate the buyer (or investor) on a great decision they won't regret and get the paperwork ready for signing.

Stick to this sales plan and you should be able to sell a dog to the cat lady across the street.

- Key points to make that sale:
    - Don't ever try to sell anything
    - Tell it as a story
    - Keep it simple
    - Offer only two or three options
    - Know your customer
    - Know your product or service
    - Don't ever lie
    - Assume the sale
    - Close the deal – don't keep selling if you already have an offer

Trust the Experts

"So much of what we call management consists of making it difficult for people to work."
                                             -*Peter Druker*

This chapter's topic is one that isn't limited to entrepreneurs; it can also help even a manager at a large corporation. Here we delve into the reasons why it's important to let the experts handle certain tasks. For example, if you've never filleted a pufferfish (fugu) for your weekly sushi soiree, you'd probably leave it to a sushi chef and trust, without hesitation, that he would do it correctly. So why do so many entrepreneurs and managers insist on doing certain skilled tasks themselves rather than hiring someone who is an expert at that task?

Some *do* hire someone, but then micromanage that person like putting a magnifying glass to an ant and end up creating a very sour relationship - or destroying the working relationship altogether.

The saying goes, "If you build it, they will come." But when they come, what will you do? There comes a time in the life of all successful small businesses when the owner can't handle all the tasks herself. Most try, because hiring someone is a big decision and can be very costly; but in the end, running all aspects of the business is unrealistic and impossible for a single person. The following article I wrote for one of my blogs will put this into perspective for you:

<u>Learn to Trust the Experts</u>

Many years ago, I had a friend who opened a women's gym in a relatively small town. He had moderate success, even though he would never become wealthy running just one gym. He later admitted that he'd opened the gym to try and meet beautiful women (which is just as stupid a reason as you can imagine for going into business). Anyway, he wanted to cut costs as much as possible, so he taught all the classes, and he handled all of the departments in the gym - like accounting, inventory, legal, etc.

I'm sure you probably already know where I'm going with this, and you may think that you would not commit these mistakes yourself, but sometimes the reality of running a small business is that you have to wear all the hats if you can't afford to have someone else wear them. In a bout of desperation, you may choose to go the cheap way and do everything yourself. ***Avoid the temptation!***

The first thing to ask yourself if faced with this issue of having to do everything yourself is, *did I plan for this in my business plan?* If your answer is no, then you *need* to go back and spend several hours or days researching and planning for this. This is not easy, as your mind and ego (we all have them!) will try and convince you that you can do it, no sweat. Take the time to research the position you're planning to take on – what responsibilities and skills will be needed.

A good method of getting quick answers for this is to look on job boards. So, for example, if you're planning on handling your own accounting, look on accounting job boards and find out what you need to know for the position. Learn about SAP, AP, AR, Payroll, Taxes, etc.

After you've researched these things, honestly ask yourself if you'd feel comfortable going on an interview for one of those positions you saw online. If your answer is no, or you have a doubt as to whether you could answer any questions the prospective employer would ask you, then you're not ready to handle that skill.

The second thing you'll need to do is ask yourself if you have enough time to handle all the tasks. My women's gym friend was teaching aerobics, cardio kickboxing, basic yoga, and doing personal training, but he also had to handle inventory, accounting, cleaning, legal, marketing, management, reports, and general clerical (like contracts!), as well as IT and maintenance for the equipment. Realistically, he couldn't handle all of that by himself in a 24-hour day without doing a crappy job on most of them.

Finally, you need accept the reality of your situation and suck it up; some of the skilled jobs need to be handled by someone else. The low-skill stuff, like cleaning, you'll need to do yourself. That's easy. But if you're not a natural manager, or an accountant, or you don't know all the laws in your municipality (city, county, state, etc.), *hire someone to do it*. And it's extremely important to remember to let go and trust your people - <u>always</u>. Don't hire someone if you're going to micromanage them, because that would completely defeat the purpose and it will take up more of your time than if you had done the work yourself.

So drop that magnifying glass and let the worker ants do what they do best. Ernest Hemmingway once said, "The best way to find out if you can trust somebody is to trust them."

Think of the business like a music ensemble: you need to focus on your instrument and trust that each of the other members of the band will perform at their best with what *they* know.

Or, the best way to think of this is like your body. If your brain had to keep up with every aspect of your being, you wouldn't last a day in this world. Your brain (manager) knows that the lungs will breathe on their own, your heart will beat like it needs to, and when you're riding a bike your legs will pedal without your brain having to micromanage any of these tasks. Your business is an entity in the eyes of the law – make sure it operates like one.

*   *   *

One of the things that many business owners feel queasy about at times is determining how much to pay their employees; always remember the old adage that says, "you get what you pay for."

Thus it is important to ensure that you pay at least what's fair and customary or perhaps even a little more if you want the best employee for a particular position.

To determine what is fair and customary for any given position you simply need to do a little bit of research. Don't just do a web search; instead, go on job websites and find a few employers who are looking to fill a similar position. Then call all of them and find out how much they are offering as a salary.

Sometimes this is easier said than done; not all employers will discuss salary until they interview the candidate and are ready to make an offer. But some will, so be persistent and insistent. You have nothing to lose by asking up front. Something along the lines of, "To avoid wasting both our times, what is the salary range you are offering for this position?"

Spending a little bit of time doing this can prove to be invaluable when you begin looking for a candidate.

And once you find a good candidate, you must be ready and willing to negotiate.

Depending on what you found during your research, you can determine if the candidate is highly qualified for the position or merely meets the minimum requirement. If it's the former, then you should be prepared and willing to land somewhere on the higher end of the spectrum. If it's the latter, then you can rest easy offering something at or near the bottom.

*   *   *

On the other side of the spectrum of doing everything yourself and not trusting your employees is having your employees do everything. This is a trap that some business owners fall into, because they've given themselves a title like CEO or President, and they feel that all tasks are beneath them and should thus fall to their employees.

This leads to resentment and diminishing respect for the owner, so be sure to allow your employees a view into what you do every day – and also regularly let them know that they are doing a great job if they really are.

Another risk of having employees do everything is that one employee will naturally rise to become a leader of sorts to the others. This leader may end up doing everything themselves; but beware! Becoming too dependent on any one employee can be disastrous to your business.

In a later chapter ("Daily Operations") we discuss in detail about employees having no clear job description and having employees who do too much. But for now, you need to know that if you depend completely on a single employee and that employee one day decides he or she doesn't want to do as much work anymore – or worse, decides to quit or take a job somewhere else – you will find yourself doing *all* the work *yourself*. If you have not performed any of those tasks in the past, you will make mistakes.

Even if you have done those tasks in the past, you will become overwhelmed if you have not been doing much work and suddenly now have to pick up a large workload – and you will make mistakes.

The worst scenario in a case where the employee does it all is if you are left suddenly lost regarding the status of your business. If you don't know your best customers, or you don't know who owes money, or you don't know which bank to deposit money into, you will basically need to start as if it was day one.

*   *   *

Perhaps the single-hardest thing for a manager or owner to do during the course of business is firing employees. This is especially true in small- and medium-sized businesses, because employees and management become very close very quickly.

However, it is imperative that no matter how close you are to an employee or how bad you feel for them because they have a sad situation at home, if an employee is not fit for the position and you can't fit them elsewhere without that person resenting you, then you have to make the tough choice.

Remember that this is your business, your livelihood. Your own family, your own financial situation, can suffer if your business fails. If an employee is not pulling their weight, then they are dragging the caravan down with them.

Think of a ship towing another, smaller ship. If the smaller ship begins to sink, you may attempt to save it, but if all efforts fail and the ship continues to sink, the ship towing it will eventually be anchored down in place. This could be your business if you keep employees who are not doing their part.

If an employee needs to be fired, sit down and think about the situation. If thoughts of that employee becoming homeless or their family being destitute start to creep into your head and you feel tempted to give the person another chance, turn your thoughts to yourself. Who will give you or your business or your family a second chance if the business fails? And if your business fails, that person will still be out of a job anyway.

The key here is to avoid giving yourself too much importance in the life of another person; you are not God. You are not the only person responsible for that person's well-being. Don't put it off until it's too late; a bad employee can ruin your business faster than you think. So do what Mark Twain says and eat that frog.

Key points to help find the person who can fold your laundry just right:
- Don't overwhelm yourself with too much work
- If it's a skilled task, hire an expert or learn the skill properly
- Do you have enough time to handle all aspects of the business yourself?
- Look on job boards to see what the task entails
- If you don't feel comfortable going for an interview for an accounting, management, HR, training, engineer position, etc. then don't assign yourself to that position – hire an expert
- Negotiate "fair" salaries for all employees
- Let employees know if they're doing well
- Don't have your employees do everything
- Don't become dependent on any single employee
- Give employees clear job descriptions
- If an employee isn't working out and you don't feel they can perform a different task, don't be afraid to terminate him or her

The Devil You Know
(Is the Same One I Know)

"Family love is messy, clinging, and of an annoying and repetitive pattern, like bad wallpaper."

-PJ O'Rourke

I've had many people ask me over the years if going into business with friends and family is really such a bad idea. And, despite my own history with this very topic, I have considered the "better a devil you know than one you don't" thing, but I've always come up with the same conclusion.

In this chapter we discuss why it's never a good idea to go into business with friends and family, and what you can do if you've already made this monumental mistake. In the next few pages we explain the many reasons to avoid mixing business and family, including several real-world examples.

Going into business with family is great - unless you're looking to grow. Family businesses are fine, if you just want to earn a living: think of Dad's Shop, O'Malley Family Restaurant, or Dad and Sons Moving. If you want to start the next Starbucks or McDonald's, it's important to know that having friends and family run an aspect of your business just because you want them involved or because you think it'll be cheap labor, then you need to go back to page 53 and read "Trust the Experts".

Family businesses only succeed when the owners make sure everyone is on the same page, has the same goals, and that there are contracts in place - or at least roles are explicitly defined in the company manual or business plan.

It should be no secret that loving your business too much can be problematic, as this can hinder your thought process when it comes to allowing your baby to "leave the nest". This is an important thing to always keep in mind, because many entrepreneurs have a hard time "letting go" and sometimes forego significant opportunities for growth because they are hesitant to give up even a small amount of equity, or they don't want to lose control of the decision-making process. There are many of us who don't have this problem, but who also have a hard time "letting go" in a different way. I'm talking about you, as the entrepreneur, allowing *yourself* to leave the nest.

I know it's extremely tempting to keep family and friends as close as possible to assist you in launching your business. After all, *better the devil you know than one you don't*, right?

Unfortunately, when it comes to business, almost all great entrepreneurs will tell you the same thing: *don't go into business with friends and family*. There are many reasons for this old adage.

From my personal experience, I know how complicated this can be. I made the mistake once of going into business with my fiancée. I thought that, since marriage is for life, this would not be an issue. Boy, was I wrong.

Our relationship quickly deteriorated; not because of the business, but because of other issues that are not relevant here. Suffice it to say, when the writing was on the wall and time came to decide how we were going to handle running the business together, it became a very delicate situation. Ultimately, I decided to cut my losses and move on; I left the business to her, but I kept many of the debts.

So, if my story is not enough to detract you from making the same mistake, consider this:

First, like with going into business because you like the product more than you like money (see the first chapter), running a business with family can blind you to issues with your friend or family member's performance. It is very easy to look the other way when a minor transgression occurs, when performance is lacking, or when the person is just a screw-up. Don't fool yourself into thinking that because the person is a good employee somewhere else, they will do well as your partner or employee; the sad fact is that many people are not cut out to be entrepreneurs, and behavior on the job will reflect this attitude. The friend or family member may take you for granted as well and may not put in 100% effort into their daily work.

I always think of "Iron" Mike Tyson, who, after spending some time in prison for rape, tried to make a comeback in the boxing ring. He had with him at ringside a bevy of friends – his entourage – who were obviously there simply for the bragging rights and prestige of being with one of the greatest boxers to ever play the sport.

However, when Mike Tyson began to lose his match, these guys looked like drunken sailors getting off a boat during a storm: they didn't know what to do to help their fighter turn the bout around, and he lost. Don't let that be your business.

Second, there is a risk of you having to discipline or worse, fire, your loved one. If this is the case, reprimanding the person will be one of the most difficult things you may ever have to do, and if you do it, it may strain your relationship. This can cause a permanent rift between you and your loved one. Remember that, especially if you're the person's boss, they often *expect* you to give them special treatment. Think of all the times you've seen, in person or on TV, someone say, "my brother owns this place. Get out," or, "my father owns this hotel chain. Go screw yourself."

This can leave a very bad stain on your business's reputation with customers or the public in general. And although many people say there's no such thing as bad publicity (we'll discuss this in a future chapter), you need to be fully aware that there is. You don't want to be known as the business owner who hires family members that are abusive to customers or other employees.

Furthermore, if you decide to discipline or terminate the business relationship with this person, they may take it as a personal assault. The person may become vindictive, destructive to your business, or worse. Don't ever underestimate how someone you love and think you know would react if they feel you've betrayed them.

Third, there is the problem of money. Nothing can tear even the most tightly-knit family apart quicker than a fight over money. Money decisions, business decisions, and more, can become a point of contention if you own a larger share of the business than your loved one. Some people will also suspect that you're not being completely honest regarding the business finances even if there's no skullduggery going on. Anything can set off these beliefs in a person; whether it's a dream, advice from another friend, or a book or TV show the person sees.

It's extremely important to always hire the right person for the job, and that may well be your loved one. If he or she is an accountant, they may be willing at first to go into it with you and handle your finances. But trust me when I tell you that there will come a time when that person thinks you're pulling a fast one on them or that you're not paying them what you would pay somebody else.

Finally, remember that you're in this to make a future for *yourself*. Your loved one may take this as a fun ride to go along with you on and may not take it as seriously as you do. They may want to impress their friends and offer them free or discounted product. Whatever happens, the most likely outcome – one I would put all my money on – is that either your relationship or your business will become a casualty. Maybe even both.

So, if you haven't gotten the point of this chapter yet, it's *don't ever go into business with family or friends – the "Devil You Know Principle" works backwards in entrepreneurship.* If you do decide to go into business with a friend or family member, plan ahead for these issues by: having an escape/action plan set; drawing up a contract for the partnership; and discussing the possibility of a future need to end the business relationship before you dive into the madness.

If you've already gone into business with a loved one, it's not too late to have a serious heart-to-heart and address these concerns with him. Get lawyers involved to ensure the terms of the agreement are fair for everyone and remind your loved one that business is business. But if after reading this you're still not convinced it's a bad idea to mix business and blood, watch "The Godfather" all the way to the end. Really, do it.

- Key point:
  - Don't go into business with loved ones
  - If you already did, make a plan, have a chat, and draw up contracts
  - Have lawyers draft contracts to ensure everything is done fairly and legally

Value Meals vs. Company Values

"Values are like fingerprints. Nobody's are the same, but you leave them all over everything you do."

-Elvis Presley

Some entrepreneurs start their companies on a whim and just go wherever the winds take them. Some plan in such detail that it makes you wonder how they ever got out of the planning stage and into real life. Most, however, whether improvisers or planners or in-betweeners, miss a very important component of a company's operational design. I'm talking about **values**.

Some managers think they know what their company's values are, while most employees will admit that they have no clue what their company's values are. Most owners, however, assume that *all* employees know – which is a very dangerous game to be playing, to make this kind of assumption with your company.

In this chapter we discuss **company values** and why they are so important to your operation. We also list five steps you can take to establish your company values and ensure employees are in line with these at all times. You can get this done rather quickly, even if your company has been in operation for a while.

Recently I was driving around with my family on a Sunday - on our way to the park - when we thought, "Hey, we've never eaten at Chick Fil-A; why don't we grab food there to take to the park?"

Unfortunately for us, Chick Fil-A doesn't open on Sundays – they never have, and probably never will. This is part of their company values, much like southern supermarket chain Publix closes on every major holiday (like Thanksgiving) to give their employees time to spend with their families – all at the expense of the company's own bottom line.

Now, if you've been reading carefully, you know I'm a huge proponent of fattening the bottom line as a sign of success in business; however, I am also a big proponent of ensuring your company is not a robotic profit machine. In the end, it's humans who keep the company alive, and humans who can end its run. So a company must have clearly defined values that will aid it in times of controversy, times of financial famine, and times of crisis. These values can serve as a company's competitive advantage (which we'll discuss in more detail in a later chapter).

I recently tried to rent a car at an airport and ran into a very common occurrence – the rep who was checking me into the car tried to scare me into buying the supplemental insurance. I've worked in the rental car industry before so I know how this works, and as a test I told the girl "just give me the basic insurance."

What many people don't know about the rental car industry is that there are usually three insurance products offered, but most people will really only benefit from one – the damage waiver, or collision damage waiver (CDW). The other two are usually liability protection (which most people already have with $0 deductible through their own insurance), and personal injury protection. However, when a customer says, "I'd like the basic insurance," many of the reps, being hungry sales people that they are, have turned semantics into a cash cow. You see, "basic insurance" to one person may mean "Damage Waiver and Injury Protection", while to another it may mean "just Damage Waiver".

This girl at the airport tried to slam me with both Damage Waiver and Personal Injury Protection. I called their corporate office later to report the behavior, and they assured me they would address the issue. However, I know their reply to me was simply a formality, as it's part of their company culture to try to maximize profitability from every rental, at any cost.

So here's why this should matter to you or your company: as in the case of the rental car company, many businesses turn a blind eye to behaviors from their employees – at every level, from front-line to upper management employees – and that behavior becomes one of the values of the company, albeit an unofficial one. If this happens within your company, customers and the public at large will judge you and your conglomerate by this behavior. This is not a good thing because a customer who feels they have no choice but to "grin and bear" the circumstances they see as unscrupulous will jump ship and swim to the competition as soon as the competition's engine is within earshot.

In the early 2000's there was a surge of this type of behavior in the wireless phone industry, as new technology came into play with wireless devices. There was now text messaging, then multimedia messaging, data plans, Ringback Tones and other upsells that provided sales reps with a nice spiff – the problem was that many consumers, when purchasing a new phone, didn't know what any of these things were, nor did they use them. There was a point where almost every person with a cellphone had a Ringback Tone (remember the, "Please enjoy the music while your party is reached"?), roadside assistance, and a text messaging plan of at least 250 messages per month.

I had several fights with salespeople and customer service representatives to get some of these unwanted charges removed, and it was definitely a major factor in my decision-making every time I had to sign a new cellphone service contract. That is until I realized that this was an industry-wide problem, not specific to any one company. See, like the rental car industry, bad company values can become a virus and spread beyond just your company – but once you have a negative reputation it's very difficult to change people's perceptions.

What are some examples of values? If you own a pet food store, you may choose to sell only all-natural, limited-ingredient food; if you run a clothing manufacturing firm, you may want to avoid sweatshops and have all your inventory made in the ol' U.S. of A.; if you run a female-friendly gym, you may offer free daycare or free Lamaze classes; you may have employees volunteer with nonprofit companies once a month; if you run a customer service call center, you may have rules allowing reps to take more than just two restroom breaks per 8-hour shift. Your values make your brand unique, like they make people individually unique.

Now - what if your employees can name McDonald's Value Meals quicker than they can name your company values? What can you do to define your values and ensure your employees abide by them?

- o First, your company needs to create a list of values. This list must be easy to read and understand, and it must be prominently displayed so that all employees can see it at all times.
- o Your values must be enforced. Punishment is never as effective as positive or negative reinforcement, so instead, try to reward employees who live by these values. Whether it is monthly with honorable mentions via mass email or in a company newsletter, or even daily with a program like Kudos Points (Kudos.com), these rewards serve to reinforce what your

company feels is appropriate behavior that is in line with its values.
- Do not waver. Like Chick Fil-A, sticking to your values - even if it means fewer profits - will eventually translate into more success. Chick Fil-A has received a lot of publicity as a result of their Sunday policy, and because of their religious agenda, and it has actually helped the company grow. This is not to mean that you should inject your religious beliefs into your company, but rather create an environment and value system, and even a company culture that customers become familiar with, so that even if you sell your company or go public the new leadership will not want to change these values; they would already be synonymous with your brand.
- Make sure your employees know your company values. The easiest way to determine this? Ask your employees If they know them. If not, it's time to make it a point to instill these values or reiterate them more frequently.

- Make sure management understands and enforces your company values. If the preacher doesn't follow his own gospel, then why should the parishioners?

With these five simple steps, your company should have a very solid base of values by which it operates. Companies that do not have a strong set of values usually pay the price in the end, whether it be because of lawsuits for unscrupulous behavior by employees or management, or simply by a loss of business from customers or clients. Values are the soul of a company, and just like a human can't function in society without a soul, neither can a company.

- Key points to guide you away from being unscrupuliscious:
    - Most managers think they know their company's core values
    - Most employees admit they don't know their company's values
    - Most owners assume all employees know and abide by the company's values
    - Values must be defined, or you risk unscrupulous behavior
    - List your values and display them prominently
    - Enforce your values
    - Live by your values
    - Make sure employees live by your values
    - Make sure management understands and reinforces your company values

Have a Vision...

"The most pathetic person in the world is someone who has sight but no vision."
                                        -Helen Keller

When you go into business, it's never because one day you decided it would be cool to start a company; there was a reason, a goal, or a result you wanted to achieve with doing so. It really baffles me sometimes how many entrepreneurs fall into the daily grind, working day in and day out, simply following the motions of the daily operation of their business. These people had a plan, even if it was just in their mind, when they opened the business, and now they just push to get through the day.

Please don't allow yourself to become that business owner; these are the type of people who become complacent and make their business a job, rather than an investment.

You, as a business owner, should have a clear idea of what you want to achieve with the company and you should strive daily to get to that point. If you are in the planning stages of your business, take the time now to think about what you want to achieve with this company. Think (realistically) about where you'd like the company to be in five, ten, twenty, and fifty years. Think, also, about where you personally want to be in those time frames. Write those things down.

If you already have a business, start by thinking about the day you started it. How many employees did you have? How much money or debt did your company have? How large was your operation (in terms of physical size, geographically, and also demographically)?

Write these down and then do the same for your situation at five, ten, twenty, and fifty years. Then, starting at your current position, think about the future, and do the same thing for the next five, ten, twenty, and fifty years.

Don't worry at this point about how you will achieve these goals; this is simply for you to think critically about what your goals are for your business and for you personally as an entrepreneur.

As an example, I'll use a rock band. Let's say Johnny, a bass player, wants to start a band. Johnny is starting this band because he wants to be a famous rock star. That's his *ultimate goal*. So, in the next five years, he plans to be able to play regular gigs in his city (Chicago) every week. He does, after all, work a full-time job currently.

In the next ten years, though, he plans on his band being so popular he can start touring the country with other small acts. He can then quit his job and play music full-time, and his band would have five albums, and maybe have his video play on MTV (does MTV still play videos?). He plans on having t-shirts and posters available at his gigs.

In twenty years, he plans on being able to headline shows across the country and have at least 12 albums out. He plans on having merchandise like t-shirts and posters, as well as other branded merchandise, available for sale through major retailers like Spencer's gifts, Amazon.com, and Wal-Mart.

In fifty years, his legacy is solidified. Johnny'll be retired and maybe do a reunion tour with surviving members of his band for their fiftieth anniversary. He may even have a televised event on HBO.

Are Johnny's goals realistic? Sure, why not. With the right connections, good music, and dedication, Johnny's band can become the next Beatles or Rolling Stones. Did he have the delusional idea that he would have an HBO Special and sell out arenas within five years of starting this band? No.

It may seem ludicrous to some of us to even think of that, yet many entrepreneurs start a business and believe that their product or service is so good that they'll reach Wal-Mart levels in no time at all. This type of unrealistic goal will lead you to make bad decisions and can cost you your entire business. I'm not saying that you can't aim to be the next Wal-Mart; just the opposite. If you don't plan on having your company grow to Wal-Mart levels, then your investors should be worried – and you should, too. The question is *when* you think you could realistically reach that level of achievement.

Once you've determined the future of your company it should be rather easy to determine which path you should take to get there. Knowing where the finish line is at each step of the company's life will help you make better decisions that will get you there.

*   *   *

Whether you already have a company up and running or are still in the planning stages of the business, one of the first things you'll need to do is create a Vision Statement. Along with the Mission Statement, this document should be used to guide your decisions throughout the life of the business and can help guide investors and managers as well.

Your Vision Statement should be clear and concise; try to keep it to one paragraph; maybe a sentence or two long.

Thus, your Vision Statement should clearly define where your company plans to be or what it plans to accomplish in the future – its *ultimate goal* - in very concise terms. For example, Google's Vision Statement is "To develop the perfect search engine", while Amazon.com's Vision Statement is, "To be the Earth's most customer-centric company; to build a place where people can come to find and discover anything they might want to buy online."

If you looked up Amazon.com's Vision Statement 20 years ago, you might find something completely different because the company started as a used book marketplace. As the business evolved into other areas, their Vision Statement evolved – and thus your company's Vision Statement may change over time as well.

Bruce Lee once said, "A goal is not always meant to be reached; it often serves simply as something to aim at."

Your company's Vision Statement, like Google's, may be something that can't really be achieved, although it guides your daily operation in the pursuit of this goal.

To create a good Vision Statement for your company be sure that you have a clear idea of your company's future aspirations. Make sure that the statement isn't vague, but also that it isn't too specific; for example, if you run a steak distribution company, you don't want to have a Vision Statement that says, "Our vision is to consistently distribute 1,000,000 steaks per year across the United States." Instead, a better Vision statement might be, "Our vision is to be the #1 steak distributor in the United States."

Of course, once this goal is achieved, your vision may evolve to include the entire western hemisphere or even the world. Once that's achieved, your vision may include distribution of food in general instead of just steak, or maybe even be as broad a statement as to include *all* perishables.

Be sure that, upon reading your Vision Statement, an investor, customer, or employee will know exactly why your company is in business – what it will be or do in the long-run. I recommend you read the chapter on Mission Statements next to help clarify the difference between a Vision Statement and a Mission Statement.

Your Vision Statement:

- Your Vision Statement should be concise
    - One paragraph, one to two sentences long
    - It should be clear
    - It should convey your ultimate goal for the future
- The statement should guide your decision-making
- It should change very little over short periods of time but can be drastically different after many years

...and a Mission

"The race is not always to the swift nor the battle to the strong, but that's the way to bet."
        -Damon Runyon

I love that quote. It highlights the insurmountable risk a challenger takes when entering a battle in which he is the underdog. As an entrepreneur, you're usually going into a battlefield of opponents who are much stronger (larger) and faster than you; they may have more customers, lower costs, or a more efficient process. But even though the odds are against you, if you are persistent and they get complacent, you can win and become larger or stronger or faster.

Your company's Vision is to win that battle and become the best; but the Vision doesn't tell your people how you will get there. Your company's Mission is that battle plan.

Many people often confuse a Company Vision with a Company Mission. The distinction is not always very clear, but there is a stark difference between the two.

A Vision Statement defines *the ultimate goals* of the company.

A Mission Statement defines why the company is in business *right now*.

Here are two examples:

"To organize the world's information and make it universally accessible and useful."

This is Google's Mission Statement, and it guides the deals they make, the technologies they research and develop, and the causes they support. If you step back, you can see that Google's Mission Statement clearly defines who they are right now.

"As a leader in communications, Verizon's mission is to enable people and businesses to communicate with each other. We are also committed to providing full and open communication with our customers, employees, and investors."

Verizon Wireless's Mission Statement is also very clear and absolutely defines who they are *at the moment*.

Because of the very nature of the Mission Statement, it should be clearly understood that the company's Mission may change regularly. For example, Amazon.com started as a used book marketplace: people bought and sold used books on the site. As the company expanded to include electronics, food items, household cleaners, clothing, and more, their mission expanded to include these things. They want to be able to provide whatever you're looking for through their website or one of its affiliates.

Sometimes a company's mission may change drastically overnight. Take, for example, the not-for-profit organization March of Dimes. This was founded in 1938 originally in large part by Franklin D. Roosevelt (partly why his face is on the American dime still today) to combat polio epidemics in children across the country.

In 1958, twenty years after its creation, the March of Dimes's Mission had been accomplished: a poliovirus vaccine had been created and found to be safe. Suddenly, the organization's mission had to be changed, and became more general - to fight birth defects. This announcement appeared to many as an overnight change in the company's focus, but the reality is that the board members and leaders within the organization had been planning for years what the organization would do once a cure for polio was found.

Your own company needs to have a plan in place as well for a "best case scenario" such as this, but we'll discuss that in more detail in the chapter on creating a business plan. For now, this example highlights the importance of taking the time to carefully craft your company's Mission Statement – and ensuring that it is not too specific or achievable. Your Mission Statement needs to be something that your employees can strive for, and something they can accomplish every day without making your company obsolete.

On the other hand, making your Mission Statement too vague can cause confusion or even distrust for your employees, customers, and investors.

Let's look at an example: "Our Mission is to be coolest car company out there."

This statement is so vague that anyone reading would be confused as to what "coolest" means. Is it literal? How do you measure "coolness"? Where is "there"? People who read this wouldn't even know where this company does business.

Of course, this may seem exaggerated, but I have actually seen Mission Statements similar to this one.

How about this one: "Our Mission is to appeal to more customers every day through positive interactions and by providing quality products that are both innovative and stylish."

Note that the words "innovative" and "stylish" are organic because they are relative to the time period in which they are used. What was stylish or innovative in the 1980's is not stylish or innovative today. So, this statement is specific, yet vague enough to allow the organization to continue doing business in a specific way.

With this example, if an investor asks your company to manufacture low-cost vehicles to widen its customer base, you can look back at this Mission Statement and see that "low-cost" is not part of the company Mission and agreeing to a decision like this could ruin your company once customers and employees begin to question why this decision was made in the first place.

Imagine Mercedes-Benz suddenly decided to sell cars to compete with low-cost Korean cars like Hyundai and Kia under their own Mercedes-Benz brand. This move would de-value the original luxury brand, and it will fail because customers will have a perception that, because these are Mercedes-Benz branded cars, they will be expensive and high-quality. There is no benefit to making this kind of decision for a company like Mercedes-Benz.

Or imagine Maruchan, a manufacturer of instant ramen noodles (the staple food of poor college students), suddenly releasing a premium "Cup-o-Noodles" that costs seven to eight times more than their traditional bargain soups. It would cause confusion, and customers may start to think the company is either desperate or it's getting greedy. This product would also fail.

Many companies that fail do so because they don't have a clear Mission Statement and their owners make decisions that baffle their customer base, or simply go against what the company represents. Remember that companies are separate entities that take on a life of their own no matter how you think you've shaped it as the owner.

Creating a Mission Statement is important because it not only conveys your company's purpose to customers, employees, and investors, but it also helps to remind you, the owner, of what the company is about. If you'd like to corner a market like low-cost automobiles when you already have the premium or luxury automobile market cornered, you can start a subsidiary or a different brand altogether. It's like Lexus and Toyota, Ford and Jaguar, Honda and Acura, or Nissan and Infinity; each of those brands, although affiliated, has its own separate Mission Statement and process, people, product, structure, and customer base.

A Mission Statement:

- Defines why the company is in business right now
- Guides your company to achieve its Vision
- Deviating from your mission can cost your company dearly
- Remember that you can always create a separate brand or subsidiary if your next venture does not fit within your company's Mission

Go on the Journey

"Aim for the sky, but move slowly, enjoying every step along the way. It is all those little steps that make the journey complete."
-Chanda Kochhar

When you set out to do something - anything - it's important to know why you're doing it and how you're going to achieve it. In business, this is not any different; you need short-term and long-term goals for your company, and every day that you operate should bring you a step closer to achieving one or more of those goals.

Many entrepreneurs, however, forget this crucial step in planning for their business. Some get caught up in the novelty of having a business of their own and make mistakes that instead end up costing them the entire business.

I would have to say that it is very tempting once you have a brand or business cards or a sign or a listing in the directory to want to have more. Believe me when I tell you (especially if it's your first company) that you'll want more: you'll want to see people wearing your t-shirts around town; you'll want to see a billboard off the expressway with your advertisement on it; you'll want to see your company mentioned in the newspaper.

Yes, people walk around with t-shirts with the "Ford" logo on it (and the person *paid* for it). Yes, billboards keep Coca-Cola at #1 in the soft drink business. And yes, Tesla seems to be in the news almost daily. These things will all come if you want them and work hard; but no matter what, you need to avoid taking shortcuts at all costs.

There once was a guy named Dick whom I consulted that had decided in the mid 2000's that cellphones were the next big thing; LG was about to release the "Chocolate" and media and messaging were very profitable after the success of the Motorola Razr. Dick opted to purchase a franchise for a Verizon Wireless Authorized retailer but made a grave mistake.

Initially, he opened his first location and did very well. It was not a huge success by any means, but he received residuals on every new and renewed contract he got customers to sign, as well as for every data, text, and supplemental plan he sold to customers. He also received a lot of support from the parent company (the franchisor) and from Verizon Wireless themselves because of the agreement he had signed.

See, he was in the books to open seven (7) locations within two years; so, a few months after opening his first location, Dick signed a lease and began work to outfit his second.

A month or so into construction, Dick had to default on his new lease and then closed his first store overnight. This was completely unexpected and was a total surprise to me and to his six employees. The customers he had from this first store made trips out to test out new phones or buy accessories, and some even to get some assistance with their accounts, only to find a vacant space in the shopping strip where the store once stood. So why did Dick fail so terribly and so quickly when he was doing so well?

The problem is that Dick didn't plan on going on a journey of growth; rather, he wanted instant gratification and aggressively tried to open all seven locations in short order. I later found out that he had never worked in the wireless phone industry before and that he had signed lease agreements for two other stores when he signed the lease for his second. He was committed to paying rent at those locations even though he wasn't making any money at them yet. He had effectively built the boat upside down in the water.

Dick wasn't honest with me or with his employees, and he kept his financials close to his chest. He lied to Verizon and to his franchisor. But worst of all, Dick wasn't honest with himself about what his goals were, nor did he have realistic ones.

Dick should have done more research about the industry in which he was going to do business; he should have made a business plan; he should have made a Mission Statement and a Vision Statement; he should have had clearly defined goals. It turns out he didn't have a business plan, and it turned out his sole investor was his father - so he didn't feel the pressure most entrepreneurs feel when they need to satisfy stakeholders.

Dick could have succeeded if he had started with one location, learned the business, proved the business concept in the demographic, and *then* had begun to research for his second location.

Remember that it is often true that, "if you build it, they will come," but there are most definitely caveats to this adage.

Walt Disney spent years scouting locations for his innovative theme park – and this was after he had already spent several years on market research to determine if a theme park based on his hit animated films would be a viable investment. He then built his park and as it achieved success, he expanded the park itself and opened other parks on the property.

Disney could easily have built an entire park based on space exploration, another based on Cinderella, another based on pirates, another based on Peter Pan, and another based on Dumbo from the start – but he opted to make these into small attractions in a single park because he didn't want to build the roof before he built the house.

Imagine if the Star Wars Trilogy had opened with Luke Skywalker fighting Darth Vader and the latter revealing his true identity as the "Dark Father" to Luke; cut to Luke fighting Vader again and defeating both him and the Emperor. Who would then care to watch the rest of the movies? Everyone who watches Star Wars for the first time knows that Luke will eventually win – that's just how stories are – but nobody sees the big twist coming, nor do they know what the final battle would be like. So why begin with the ending and leave nothing for the viewer to look forward to?

Thus, if you begin at the end – especially in business – you leave nothing for investors, customers, or even yourself to work toward, and you are guaranteed to fail. Remember Amazon? They didn't start as a retailer for everything under the sun; this was achieved over many years and through various acquisitions.

Another great example is Marvel Studios and DC Films. In 2008, Marvel Studios released *Iron Man* and after the success of that movie they released several other movies, including *The Incredible Hulk*, *Thor*, and *Captain America: The First Avenger* before deciding to release *Marvel's The Avengers* to massive success, as well as ultimately launching a new appreciation for comic books and superhero films.

DC Films, however, took a different approach. They released *Superman Returns* and *Batman v. Superman* and then *Wonder Woman* just before *Justice League* – and they failed to introduce three of the main characters that would appear in that film or proving that audiences even cared about these characters teaming up. There was no hype, no tension built up, and no ultimate goal, because they began with it: the plan from the beginning was to make a *Justice League* movie.

Keep in mind that your company will most likely have humble beginnings and it will most likely have very aggressive goals, but you must embrace those humble beginnings if you are not ready to run a multi-million dollar global corporation; don't get ahead of yourself, it will come.

So what kind of goals can you have as a small corporation? What about other types of companies?

A service or less tangible product such as a limited partnership - like a musical group - can continue to grow by selling merchandise as rock bands Kiss and Iron Maiden have done; both have become multi-million-dollar brands whose products are purchased by people who aren't even fans of the music. These bands have made everything from coffins to video games. A band or other service leader can also become a mentor like rapper P-Diddy did with the TV show *Making the Band* or like the hosts of *The Voice*, a competition game show hosted by famous music artists.

A YouTube channel or podcast could begin expansion by opening an online store or adding services like *The Art of Manliness Podcast* has done with their *The Strenuous Life* service or like the *Lore* podcast has done with expanding to a TV show on Amazon Prime (also titled *Lore*).

A retailer may open new locations and eventually franchise its brand; it may expand to online sales and open an eBay or Amazon store; it may expand to international markets; it can open subsidiaries for fundraising like Krispy Kreme Doughnuts has done with great success.

There are many small steps or short-term goals that can make your journey as an entrepreneur worthwhile. Without short-term goals it becomes too easy to get overwhelmed, restless, anxious, and frustrated. These feelings can lead to risky decisions and can cost you your business. The excitement of achieving a goal and having a new one to look forward to can keep that honeymoon feeling alive for you while you run your business.

A final example is one of a local breakfast and lunch spot in my city. They had a very modest 600-square foot space, and for over a year the owners, Christina and Giorgio, ran the place like true professionals. Then, because they found their restaurant packed daily, they leased the retail space next to their café when it became available to avoid having people lining up outside and risk losing customers. This expansion essentially doubled their space - and the wait staff, cleaning crew, and even the owners had that glint in their eyes like they did the first day they opened.

The next step for Christina and Giorgio is most likely to open a second location; but I'm sure they will not jump to that step until after the expansion has proven itself viable. A journey is easiest on the traveler when done in small sections – so travel light; *that's* the smart way to travel.

For your journey:

- Avoid shortcuts and instant gratification
- Take time to learn your industry
- Open only a business you can handle and prove your concept before expanding
- Don't start at the end; build up to something big
- Think of several small, realistic goals and plan for them

Fostering Your Ideas

"The difficulty lies not so much in developing new ideas as in escaping from old ones."
                                                -John Maynard Keynes

A few years ago, I turned on the television and saw an advertisement for what I thought was the most ridiculous product ever made. The ad featured a family sitting on their couch watching television wearing what looked like a thick poncho; it was a blanket with sleeves and a hole cut out in the middle of it for a person to put their head through. They called the product the "Snuggie" and the commercial made it sound like this was the greatest product ever invented.

The funny thing about this story is that, according to Yahoo Finance, the Snuggie sold over 30 million units and raked in more than 500 million dollars in revenue within its first five years of release. That's nothing to laugh about. Nor is the success of the stool designed to slide under your feet while you use the toilet - called the Squatty Potty – that has sold millions of dollars' worth of inventory. But how did they do it?

Great tongue-in cheek marketing has played a major role for both of these brands, sure. I'm sure many of their sales are actually gag gifts. However, the strength of these products has been proven over time, because unlike other gag gifts that fizzle after a few months of release, these have remained profitable for many years after they were introduced to the market.

Ingenious marketing aside, the success of these companies in general and these products specifically can mostly be attributed to the careful fostering of a unique idea. None of these products was an "overnight success"; rather, the ideas were honed and tested and carefully built upon over time until those ideas were ready for the market.

The key point here is that simply believing you have a good idea doesn't necessarily make it good. Asking your friends and family about the idea will not give you an accurate reading of how the market will react to it, either.

Take, for example, the Hollywood celebrity restaurant concept *Planet Hollywood*. Backed by several famous celebrities like Arnold Schwarzenegger and Bruce Willis, the concept was the brainchild of Robert Earl, who had been employed at concept restaurant Hard Rock Café at the time. The restaurant was almost a carbon-copy of Hard Rock Café, only with a Hollywood movie star and memorabilia theme throughout. After a successful and very publicized launch, Earl left Hard Rock Café and was subsequently sued by his former employer for trade secrets appropriation; and because of this and other reasons, the restaurant concept would end up filing chapter 11 bankruptcy twice in the next two decades.

Although Planet Hollywood ended up opening a successful hotel and casino in Las Vegas and also purchasing the Bucca di Beppo restaurant chain, the company is considered a major failure. The concept was not original – it was simply a derivative of Hard Rock Café – and the customers were not satisfied with the food nor the service.

A concept alone can't grant you success; the idea itself must be fostered into a complete business. This is why a gimmicky product will last in the market for a limited amount of time. This is why a great restaurant can still go out of business. And this is why a great company name or logo will only take you so far.

A mistake many entrepreneurs make is that they get an idea and immediately jump head first into making it a reality. Yes, the early bird gets the worm, but there's a hindrance to being the first bird on site.

In Rome, starlings flood the city in the winter season by the millions. Peregrine falcons have learned that the starlings appear during the early evening for mealtime – so the falcons wait for the birds to simply come to them as easy prey. The smart starlings have in turn learned of the falcons' plot, so they wait in groups - forming some amazing aerial displays in murmurations of thousands before finally descending for the evening meal. The starlings that are too eager and descend too early are snatched up easily by the falcons.

As a business owner, your idea needs to hang back for a little while to allow the other starlings to become falcon fodder before you set on course. Your idea needs to be ready; and the best way to achieve this is to make sure it's not alone. What I mean by this is that you shouldn't rely simply on a single idea. If the market doesn't respond well to it, you're done like those impulsive starlings.

In 1908, Sunshine Biscuits created a chocolate cookie with a crème center; they called it *Hydrox*. The cookie was rather popular – that is, until 1912, when the Oreo cookie was introduced. Oreo is currently the #1 selling cookie in America. Perhaps it was the name, perhaps the packaging, or perhaps even the marketing that cost Hydrox the title, but it's undeniable that being first is not always necessarily the best option.

Brainstorm several ideas. Dozens. Then narrow them down to the best five to ten and work on them simultaneously to ensure each is its best version before you focus group them or present them on surveys to potential customers; have professionals (like consultants) review them.

Once you have a few great ideas that seem like viable candidates, continue to fine-tune them. Then let them sit for a bit. Many writers will churn out a story in a few short minutes, then walk away for several days before revisiting it. I, for one, often find that my first draft is never anywhere near what I am initially trying to convey; even worse, I've removed from circulation most of the books I've written and self-published on Amazon because after re-reading them years later, I've realized how much more work they needed before they were ready to be published.

Don't make the mistake of allowing yourself to be wrapped up and sucked in by the whirlwind of excitement that follows the creation of an idea. Yes, it's really neat to see a "For Lease" sign on a building be replaced by a sign with your business name on it. It's an awesome feeling to see your product on a television ad. But what's not awesome is having to do a product recall due to a flaw that you didn't catch during testing because testing was rushed. Even worse is having to see your business's sign be replaced by a "For Lease" sign.

Fostering your ideas:

- Good ideas must be vetted before being presented to market
- An idea alone is not enough to bring success; the idea must be fostered into a complete business
- Don't be impulsive – let your idea simmer for a while
- Have more than just one idea; if your idea fails, you'll have more to fall back on

What Type of Company is This?

"Knowing yourself is the beginning of all wisdom."
-Aristotle

Part of creating a complete business, from forming ideas to concepts to values and more, is also being able to fully define that creation. As a business owner, you'll need to be prepared to provide a sort of ***elevator pitch*** to potential investors and customers.

In sales, an elevator pitch is a succinct sales pitch that can be presented to a prospective client while riding up ten floors on an elevator – thus, it's usually a 30-second to 1-minute long explanation of your product or service.

Similarly in the corporate world, you should be able to explain your company or business to people you meet in such a manner that it gets the point across before the person loses interest or is confused by the whole thing. Some examples of current popular companies and their elevator pitch descriptions are eBay ("an online auction site for regular people or businesses"), Home Depot ("a home improvement supply store"), or Starbucks ("a hip gourmet coffee shop"). With these descriptions you know exactly what you can and can't find at each of these – so you wouldn't walk into Starbucks expecting a steak dinner or walk into a Home Depot expecting to find reams of paper.

What happens when an organization strays from their defined capacity is it confuses consumers and it can rattle investors. Take, for example, Burger King Corporation in the early 1990's; the company introduced table service, complete with gourmet platters including shrimp and steak. The concept failed in just a few months because people did not understand what steak and shrimp had to do with Burger King or fast food.

The company tried again years later to drum up business – this time with hot dogs, chili dogs, tacos, and even pizza. The new items made Burger King's menu too big and confusing, and the company perhaps inadvertently or perhaps on purpose invited competition from Taco Bell, Nathan's Famous, and the numerous pizza chains across the country that are largely successful. As a company, Burger King had to ensure with this move that their tacos were better than Taco Bell's, their hot dogs better than Nathan's, and their pizza better than Pizza Hut – but the problem is that they weren't.

A company that tries to venture into another category or industry needs to be prepared to compete in that industry – but *before* even venturing out into other categories a company needs to be the **best** at their *primary* category.

Sure, it's rather easy to go from selling airplane parts to also selling parts for boats because it's a ***lateral move*** – but if you're not the best supplier of airplane parts or at least *one* of the best, then why bring more competition for yourself?

To keep from straying or meandering, your leadership needs to follow the company's Mission and Vision plans; that's the whole point of these two documents: they keep you grounded and keep you from making silly mistakes that can cost your company everything.

Once your brand is established, if you have an idea that doesn't fit exactly into your Mission, Vision, or brand as you've defined it then you need to formulate a plan on how you'll introduce that new idea. Korean economy car maker Hyundai created a luxury car, the *Genesis*, but nowhere on that vehicle is Hyundai's trademark logo to be found. My recommendation, however, is that you consider a creating a subsidiary or a completely separate company for the idea. Think of Honda and Acura, Nissan and Infinity, Ford and Jaguar, or even Trader Joe's supermarkets and Aldi food stores.

Alternatively, you can work backwards and create an umbrella corporation that holds various brands under it, like Johnson and Johnson, Darden Restaurants, Diageo, and General Motors.

If you haven't noticed, all of the companies I've listed are very large conglomerates. This is not to mean that a small company can't diversify in the way some of these giants have, but keep in mind that spreading yourself out too thin too early can be dangerous to your success.

Focus on your company. Once your company has grown to a satisfactory level then you can make changes, introduce new products, etc. Major changes should only occur if there is a complete necessity – such as if your original idea is failing or becoming obsolete.

However, there is a caveat. There's a difference between making a major change that completely shifts the focus of your business from its original model and making a change to simply keep up with the industry. As examples, let's take a look at some successful movie rental companies from recent decades.

Blockbuster video was a major success in the mid-1980's when Wayne Huizenga and David Cook founded the video rental superstore. The concept was so successful that the company expanded and opened Blockbuster Music, which was a record and cd store with aggressive goals for the future of digital music. Huizenga even wanted to open a Disney World-style Blockbuster theme park in Florida.

The company and management, however, was too busy looking at other ventures to see what was happening with the core business. A start-up named Netflix had just entered the market boasting no late fees, plus the convenience of receiving as many rentals in the mail per month as one wanted for a flat fee, each delivered within 2-3 days.

Simultaneously, another company named RedBox started making deals placing automated rental machines at supermarkets and drug stores. These allowed the customer to rent movies for a low price and pay a flat daily rate with no limit on the number of days - and best of all they allowed the customer to return the movie to any other RedBox kiosk in the country without incurring additional fees.

Blockbuster, being too busy with other ventures, quickly lost market share to all of these competitors. They made a desperate move by removing late fees, then implementing a subscription service that offered a flat monthly rate for unlimited rentals in their brick-and-mortar stores. Soon after that they started a kiosk rental business to try and rival RedBox, and eventually they tried a mail order service like Netflix as well. The problem was that by the time all of these were launched, the new big thing in video rental was digital streaming. It was too little too late.

Unfortunately, the story does not end there; RedBox did not learn from their competitor, Blockbuster, and stuck to the kiosk rental business. The company delayed entering the online streaming market, and they've paid the price. As of this writing, there are hundreds of streaming movie services, from Hulu to Vudu to

Netflix, which made a quick move to digital streaming and had the luck (or foresight) of having a name that is conducive to that of a streaming service; RedBox has entered the digital streaming battlefield a little too late, and unless they have a competitive advantage to overcome the other services, they will be fighting a losing battle.

So, with all of that said, I will reiterate – and I can't say it enough - remember to focus on your business. Don't let yourself get sidetracked by other ventures before you're ready; make sure you keep your eyes on the business and push it to success while staying relevant within your industry. If you get excited over a different venture, then it's time to hire a manager to run your business while you focus on the new venture.

To define your company:

- Decide on a business model and stick to it
- Have a business "elevator pitch"
- Be the best at what you do before expanding to other things
- Follow your Mission and Vision
- Consider a subsidiary or umbrella company for incongruent ideas
- Don't over-commit on major changes
- Keep up with your industry's changes to stay relevant

Play by the Numbers

"If you don't know your numbers, you don't know your business."
                              -Marcus Lemonis

Gear up, because this is going to be a very dense chapter.

From day one you should be able to spew out several statistics and numbers about your business to anyone who asks – and I'm about to reveal to you the basics of those statistics. Like with the rest of this book, this chapter is a primer; by no means is this a comprehensive look into what you will need, but it's a start. So get a pen and paper and let's get to it.

The main document all businesses utilize as a quick snapshot of their business's financial standing is the **Profit and Loss Statement (P&L)**, also known as an **Income Statement**. This takes the total expenses for the business and subtracts that figure from the gross profit to obtain the net income. It is a very basic chart that can give an investor or manager a quick idea of the health of the business at any given moment. Below is a sample P&L:

Income	
Popcorn Sales	$500
Ticket Sales	$200
Total Income	**$700**
Cost of Goods Sold	
Cost of Goods Sold	$100
Supplies and Materials	$50
Total Cost of Goods Sold	**$150**
Gross Profit	*$550*
Expenses	
Advertising	$50
Bank Charges	$25
Studio Charges	$50
Total Expenses	**$125**
Net Operating Income	*$425*
Other Income	
Interest	$25
Total Other Income	**$25**
Net Other Income	*$25*
Net Income	**$450**

It is important to note that this statement does not take into account many of the factors that a Cash Flow Statement, Balance Sheet, or ***Earnings Before Interest, Tax, Depreciation, and Amortization (EBITDA)*** do, but it is the most popular financial document to use when requesting assistance from an investor. Banks will want all of the above forms to get more detail on your business, such as fixed, variable, and periodic expenses, and specifics like operating expenses, non-operating expenses, and ***Selling, General, and Administrative (SG&A)*** costs; some investors will require these as well, so after you master the P&L, I recommend you get a finance or accounting book and learn about all of these – then apply them to your business.

* * *

When selling goods or services, there is an important word to always have in mind: margins. While standard margins vary by industry, most businesses operate at an average 15-20% margin. Ideally, a 30% margin should be the goal.

If you are not familiar with the term or have heard it but don't know how to even determine a margin, take note. It is a simple formula, but most people fail at accurately calculating their margins for several reasons. We'll get to those later, but first, the formula.

% Margin = (Gross Profit /Revenue) x 100

So if your shoes sell for $100 but the cost is $80, then your margin on those shoes would be 100-80 = 20 (gross profit);now the formula ($20/$100) x 100 gives us a total of 20%. Simple, right?

Here's where it gets tricky. Most people, when calculating a margin for a product, take only the cost of materials - say $80 for those shoes – for their calculations. There's not much wrong with that, because this gives you *Gross Margins* – but what gives you a true representation of how much money you're making is **Net Profit Margin**.

To calculate Net Profit Margin you need to take into account all of your costs for that item – including your operating costs, returns, and other expenses. Now this is where those other financial statements come in handy.

How much did your company spend on electricity? How much was spent on the lease? How much was depreciation of assets? How much were taxes? Shipping costs? Salaries? Miscellaneous expenses like toilet paper and cleaning products? What about damaged goods received? Interest on loans? Marketing?

There are so many expenses that a business has, that it cannot be assumed the business operates in a vacuum. This is why I don't like to use the Gross Margin for any of my calculations. Sure, it'll give you an accurate snapshot of what the product costs you before your ***actual expenses***. Careful, however to avoid including ***sunk costs*** – which are one-time costs that are considered settled. For example, a bike rack purchased for the RV you use for your "camping tours" business. It was a one-time expense that will not be repeated, nor does it have residual costs associated with it.

The percentage amount deducted from each individual item or service for operating expenses will vary depending on how many units or services are rendered by that business in a year. So if your business sells 100,000 books the percentage for each book to be deducted as costs will be lower than the "per-massage" cost for a company that performs 2,000 massages per year.

However, if your operating expenses are 30% or more of the cost of each product or service you offer, then you need to raise your prices.

This is why restaurants are constantly raising the price of their food items; their expenses are very high and their margins are very low (typically in the 5-15% range). It is also why restaurants are the most common business to go close shop within the first two years of operation.

But don't despair; being prepared by knowing your numbers will help you stay ahead of the pack and keep you from falling into any of those dire statistics.

On another note, there is something I like to call the raindrop effect. Even with low margins you can be heftily profitable. Think of stores like Dollar Tree, in which everything sells for $1 and has a very modest margin. Their business model relies on each customer purchasing several items at $1 each, and they have a lot of customers. This, like raindrops, adds up to a deluge of profitability under the right conditions. In similar fashion, restaurants rely on many patrons every day to turn a hefty profit.

* * *

Once you know your company's profitability and your product or service's margins, you need to determine how much your company is actually worth. If you need to go to an investor and negotiate terms based on your valuation, you need to be prepared to produce fair terms for that would benefit both parties.

Nothing turns investors off more than someone who doesn't know their numbers, and that includes knowing the true valuation of their company.

Be aware that there is no single way of valuing a company, but rather multiple methods. The most common methods are: asset-based valuation method, comparable transactions method, multiples method, DCF analysis, and market valuation.

The asset-based valuation method uses the Net Asset Value (NAV) of all the company's total assets and subtracts total liabilities. So, if a car dealership has a NAV (cars, furniture, etc) of $500,000 and liabilities (debts, etc.) of $400,000, the value of the dealership utilizing this method is $100,000 ($500,000 - $400,000).

The comparable transactions method basically compares the company in question with a similar company. Usually the company used for comparison will have similar assets and liabilities, as well as similar customer base, business model, products, and services. Keeping with the car dealership example, this would mean that our dealership can be compared to Joe's Car Shack, which recently sold to an investor for $300,000. Joe's had similar assets ($450,000), liabilities ($330,000), business model, and products and services.

Based on the sale of Joe's, our company would be valued at $300,000 as well.

In the multiples method, specific items from a financial statement are compared between two or more similar companies using a ratio. There are many variations of the multiples method, but for simplicity's sake we will use a basic example.

A computer repair company is compared with a cellphone repair company and a television repair company. These are estimated to be valued at the same level, so their financial sheets are taken for comparison.

The Estimated Value is taken for each and divided by the Total Liabilities, giving us the following:

CoR: $20,000/$40,000 = 0.50

CeR: $20,000/$70,000 = 0.29

TvR: $20,000/$32,000 = 0.63

And we can see that the TV repair company is the most valuable.

Discounted Cash Flow (DCF) analysis uses a lot of complex math to arrive at a figure, but it basically estimates the firm's future cash flow growth for several years by comparing the growth in prior years, then adjusts those future projections in today's terms using the *time value of money* (a concept in which money is worth more today than in the future).

As a very simplified example, let's say we have a lipstick company that shows past growth of 3% to 5% based on free cash flow of $20k. We calculate future growth based on free cash flow of 6% the first couple of years and 4% the next three years after that. Then we find a weighted average cost of capital which acts as the discount rate. After all calculations are complete, we find that the fair market value of the company is $300k.

I recommend looking up the formulas for the DCF so you can gain a better understanding of this analysis, because it is one of the best for investors – which may likely be what you run into when negotiating investment capital.

The final valuation model is Market valuation; market valuation determines the actual value of an organization utilizing its current stock prices.

Whichever of these methods you utilize, make sure that any assumed calculations are based on solid mathematical principles and realistic projections, rather than assumed growth based on hope or unrealistic goals.

*   *   *

Directly related to valuation comes a discussion on how to properly negotiate for capital investments based on this valuation figure. The key point of this section is that what matters is not necessarily the percentage of equity you own, it's the value of the business.

Let's take an example. You own 100% of company W. The company is worth $100, and you project your growth to be 10% per year for the next 5 years. That would mean that at the end of 5 years, you own 100% of $146.41 at year 5.

Now, let's say you own 100% of company K, also valued at $100. However, an investor makes you a deal in which she promises that your business will grow by 20% every year for the next 5 years. In exchange for this, she wants 25% of your company. This means that you'd now own 75% of company K, or $75.

However, as the years pass, your growth of 20% per year lands the company at a value of $207.36 on year 5. Although you've given up ¼ of your company, this valuation means your portion is worth $155.52 (75% of $207.36). So the investor's input, contacts, or whatever, have boosted your company's value and brought you more money with company K than you would have earned y yourself with company W.

I know those $9.11 over five years may not sound like much, but this is with a company valued at $100. If the valuation was 10,000 times that, or $1 million, you're looking at a difference of over $90,000, which could probably pay off a huge part of your mortgage or even get you that Mercedes-Benz you've always wanted.

But what if you feel your company has the potential to grow exponentially, and you want an investor's offer to reflect that? Well, this one is very simple. Think of the folksy indie singer who performs at your local coffee house and tries to give away copies of her cd, but nobody will even take them for free. The singer may have tons of talent, and she believes that if only the right producer could attend her show or listen to her cd she'd be an international star. Would you give this singer $250 for her guitar strap? I would hope not. But if this singer, two years later, turns out to be Jewel, things may be a bit different. Her sweaty guitar strap may be worth $1000 on an auction site. The rub is in that the singer has to become Jewel, which is not easy.

What all this means is, every entrepreneur believes that they have *the one*: the product, the company, the brand, etc. that will break records and make everyone involved so much money they could each purchase a tropical island. For an investor, potential means nothing. The numbers *today* are what matters, and if in your company's current situation you can't get to a Wal-Mart level of success without the help of investors, then that means the investors have the value – the value to you beyond what you may believe.

Remember that when seeking out investors your mentality cannot be one of arrogance; you're not doing the investor any favors by allowing them to give you money. This is a flawed attitude from the beginning, because remember, you came to them with hands out. Be realistic about your situation – if you can't scale your company without the help of investors, then you need to be willing to give up something valuable in exchange for the risk they are taking with you – so forget about bloated future valuation and be realistic and humble and things can be great for you.

However, do not give up more than 60% of your business the first few years of operation. Remember Wally Amos and his story. This is what is in business referred to as a ***down round*** – it's a round of investing in which the valuation of the company has been diluted so much that new investors signing on can purchase ownership of the company at lower prices than prior investors – and it's neither good for the old investors nor for the company owner.

* * *

There comes a time in the life of all businesses in which the growth just isn't what it used to be. Even the biggest and the best have fallen into this rut. Stagnant growth, however, can always be remedied if immediate and decisive action is taken.

The first step is to identify the cause of the stagnation. Look at your financial sheets and determine what's happening; is it increased costs? Lower sales? Stagnant sales? Declining production?

If it's costs, identify specific reasons. Is it salaries? Is it materials? Import duties? Shipping costs? Operational costs like lease payments?

If it's lower sales, identify why. Is it an inability to fulfill orders? Are customers leaving for the competition? Is your product or service becoming obsolete (lack of innovation)?

Whatever the reason for the stagnation, make a plan immediately to rectify it. If it's costs, look for ways to reduce these. Perhaps your commission structure is too generous. Perhaps the factory in China is charging more than one would in Taiwan. If it's import duties, is there a way to have the product made less expensively in the U.S. or Mexico?

For lower sales, find out if a special promotion would help. Perhaps a new color for the item would attract customers. Maybe the competition is offering a discount for new customers – maybe you can counter-offer by providing a discount for past customers. If your product is obsolete, brainstorm on what would put you at the forefront of the technology within the industry.

The point is that it is imperative that you nip this in the bud and act decisively. If you notice growth begin to decline or stagnate, fix it!

When it comes to stagnation, I like to think of my favorite quote from Jerome Lawrence's *Inherit the Wind*: "Maybe it's you who've moved away by standing still."

Know your numbers:

- Learn how to make and read a P&L Statement
- Know your margins
- Think of the raindrop effect if you are in a low-margin industry
- Remember the 30% rule for operational costs
- Don't base your valuation on bloated future expectations; be realistic
- Be prepared to give up equity for the right investment
- However, don't give up more than 60% of your company the first few years – you could end up diluted for future investments (down round)
- If your business growth is stagnant, identify the problem and fix it immediately

Here's the Plan

"Plans are nothing; planning is everything."
-Dwight D. Eisenhower

The core of any business – the Business Plan. Within it, your entire operation should be outlined and delineated so that if you die before your business can take flight, the executors of your estate can still launch the sucker.

The details of a Business Plan can be found in many publications and guides that focus solely on this topic. What we will be presenting here is a basic outline of your Business Plan along with a few specifics for you to consider that are most commonly missed by business owners.

In case you don't know what a Business Plan is, it's a document that contains everything about your business. Imagine you are a bank – a lender – and you want to make sure that your money will not go to waste, but rather to someone who is likely to succeed. That's what the Business Plan will relay to the lender. You can find a raw sample of a BP on my website.

The Business Plan (BP) is generally drafted before the business is launched; it is completed just before you begin seeking initial capital for your business. It can also serve you when you are seeking investment capital after you've gone into business. It's astounding how many business owners do not have a BP prepared before they venture out, and this is a big mistake.

It's no wonder why so many new businesses fail.

In fact, there is a saying that goes, "The business that fails to plan, plans to fail." Yet people still don't do it. Maybe it's arrogance or laziness, but putting in the work – which it *is* a lot of work – will take you a long, long way.

The first thing to keep in mind about a BP is that it is gonna take some time to draft. No doubt about it, it's gonna take several phone calls, some research, some deep thought, and a ton of hours. But you want to make sure that you put the time and effort into it, because if you rush it you will miss something. Believe me, my tanning salon was extremely successful because of the time I put into my BP. My nonprofit company did not do so well because I actually spent more time designing the logo than working on the BP, and it came back to bite me.

Silly as it may sound, the first thing you want to do is make sure you have your word processor properly set for your BP – nice font, nice formatting, right margins, killer title page. Remember that this is going to be seen by many important people – particularly your investors and lenders. So make it pretty!

Other than the title page, be sure to include a table of contents to make it easy to navigate the document – it may end up being several dozen pages long.

The first section should be the resumes and current credit reports of all parties involved: the owners, the executives, the managers, and any other key players for your organization; banks and investors will be much more motivated if they are able to quickly learn about all of the key players in the company at a glance. If it saves *them* time, it saves *you* time and brings you closer to a deal.

Next you will need a **Statement of Purpose**; why are you going into business and why are you seeking capital? What will the funds be used for (in general terms)?

Your **Organizational Plan** will be next, and it will contain things like a description of the business (and what industry it falls into), legal structure (non-profit, S corporation, limited partnership, etc. – more on this in a later chapter), the products and/or services that the business will offer, profiles of customers (who will purchase your product or utilize your service and why) and demographics, management and personnel (including each of their daily duties), as well as a profile of the typical employee (what traits would you look for in an employee when you begin interviewing – dependable/punctual, outgoing, dedicated to safety, etc.).

This section will also include the methods of recordkeeping (accounting, how often it will be done, in what format/software, how will it be backed up, etc.), the information for your insurance carrier (if you don't have insurance yet, list two or three potential or prospective insurers and list the details such as the deductible, liability, monthly and annual premium, and the cost of workers' compensation).

Security should also be addressed in this section, specifically the risks to security (types of internal/external theft such as cash register theft, shoplifting, falsification of signatures, identity theft, inventory shortage, robbery/break-in, etc. - and your plan on how you will be thwarting or handling it), as well as other types of loss you may think of (damage from flood, fire, etc.).

The next section should be your **Marketing Plan**, in which you list your target market. Try to list at least three targets if you can, along with who, what, where, and when. For example, customers of a local supermarket may be my first target for my beauty salon. The "who" will explain the reason they are a target – most supermarket shoppers are women and may not be aware of the existence of the salon. The "what" will state what the marketing format is – perhaps giving out a flyer during mornings and evenings when the supermarket is busiest. The "when" would list the specific times and frequency of your marketing method (weekdays and on Sundays after the local church lets out at 12:30 pm, etc.). The "where" could be the parking lot or if you've spoken with the supermarket already and received permission from management, the entryway of the supermarket.

The next section will list all competition in the nearby area if you are a brick-and-mortar location like a hot dog stand, and other opportunity buys if you are a service or product, like a clothier that has shelf space at multiple other business locations.

Next you will want to list your planned promotional activities. Examples: social media sites and how you will utilize them, magazine ads - include the complete ad information: ad size, coverage [weekly, females 25-49, in English 295,000 and in Spanish 188,000 subscribers), timing (weekly on Sundays), section (after the column titled, "Ask Jenny"), ad location, contact and fees – this will be the name and address of the publication (e.g., Vogue Magazine / Vogue en Español, $1450 per run in the page after the "Ask Jenny" column, Betty Veronican (212) 330-0997 / $750 per run in other sections, Betty Veronican (212) 330-0997)].

Be sure to list all marketing – include signage, flyers, phone book or internet ads, etc. and include pricing and what each will specifically say. Brainstorm until you have everything you will be using!

Finally, this section will include how you will track promotional activities. Perhaps you will include a discount code that identifies each, or you could use a survey (which could be verbal) to determine how the customer heard about your place. This section should also include assumptions on your returns from promotional activities. For example, 10 new customers per week for every 3,000 flyers and 15 customers per week from all magazine ads.

The next section is what your investors and financiers will be looking at most closely. It is the **Financial Documents** section.

First you should have a ***Summary of Financial Needs***. This will establish who will be signing for the loan and for what reason the loan is needed. It will also include how much capital was invested by the owners and specifically how much is needed, along with specifics on what the funds will be used for.

Following would be a ***Loan Fund Dispersal Statement***, which goes into further details still on what the funds will be used for (e.g., $3,800 for the location lease, $4,500 for equipment lease – 8 chairs, 8 lamps, and 8 commercial-grade hair dryers, $2,000 for marketing and signage, $5,000 for construction – accessibility ramp, creating a window, building a bathroom, etc.).

Next, we have a ***Back-up Statement***, which would specify how you plan to pay back the loan (e.g., "$70,000 at 9% interest for 15 years would have estimated monthly payments of $1250. A total of 6 customers per day would easily double this amount"), re-iterate how much money the owners put into the business, relist the expected address of the property if it's a brick-and-mortar, reiterate where you will be drawing your customers from, and list the deadline when you need the funds by and why ("funds needed by October 3rd, 2019 to begin construction and begin marketing for an expected opening date of November 30th. Loan repayment can begin on November 30th for a 15-year period").

You will also need to have *Financial Projections* in this section. This will include a *Pro-Forma Cash Flow Statement*, *Three-Year Income Projections*, and a *Break-Even Analysis*.

Next you should have an **Operational Plan**. This is where you will need to have your list of necessary positions and their complete job descriptions, planned daily operation (take inventory in the morning, sweep/mop floors and clean toilets, count cash register, etc.). *NOTE:* For your and your employees' safety and security, making deposits should be randomized. Nobody but *you* should know when deposits are being taken to the bank. *DO NOT* list this in the business plan, but instead figure out a way to randomize deposits so that nobody can figure out any sort of pattern.

Next you should have a plan for several different events such as disasters (fire, flood, tornado, earthquake, hurricane), riots, protests, parades, robbery, employees calling out, employees suddenly quitting, disgruntled employee/active shooter, fight between customers or employees, intoxicated patron, shoplifter, worst case scenario for your business performance, best case scenario for your business performance (if you grow too quickly), blackout/brownout, computer malfunction, and anything else you can think of. Take the time to come up with things that can become hurdles for your daily business operation. Visit other businesses; or while you're out to dinner or shopping watch carefully and take note of things that may happen in *your* business that you need to plan for – then add those plans to your BP.

Also list the goals of your business for the next 2, 5, and 10 years, what is needed to achieve them and how you plan to get there.

Finally, you need a **Supporting Documents** section. Here you can have things like case studies of other similar businesses within your industry, news articles regarding your industry, scientific studies, etc.

After doing all of this work you will feel like you've written a book (because you practically will have!) But you should feel very confident in your ability to run a successful business, or that the business will run well even in your absence. Plus, you will have a very clear picture of how you will get there, how you will market your brand, and you'll be prepared for anything life throws your way.

The Plan:

- Spend time on your BP – don't rush it, because you don't want to miss anything
- Make it look nice – this is what you will present to banks and investors when you seek capital as a new or existing business
- Include a Table of Contents
- Include the resume of all parties (owners, managers, executives, etc.) and current credit reports
- Also have:
    - A clear Statement of Purpose
    - Organizational Plan
    - Marketing Plan
    - Financial Documents
    - Operating Plan
    - Supporting Documents

Legalease

"Ignorance of the law excuses no man from practicing it."
                                                -Addison Mizner

Once you've decided that you will be going into business and created your Business Plan you need to make everything legal. To do so, you'll need to have an understanding of the different types of companies that you can have in the United States and decide on which one would best suit your needs.

A **sole proprietorship** is a type of company (usually small) in which there is a single owner who assumes complete responsibility for the organization. This includes benefits and liabilities, as well as income and obligations. A sole proprietorship is not an independent entity in the eyes of the law, so any legal liabilities are also shared by the owner.

Sole proprietorships are usually businesses like independent sales – think Avon, Mary Kay, Amway, etc. Agents for multi-level marketing companies also tend to fall into the sole proprietorship category.

For tax purposes, a sole proprietorship's earnings will be filed under the owner's tax return, and thus taxes can get rather high if the company is even moderately successful. When the income flows directly to an individual the organization is known as **flow-through entity (FTE)** or **pass-through entity**. An advantage of an FTE is that taxes do tend to be lower because the *double-tax* is avoided (the double tax is a tax on the corporation's earnings and then a taxation on employees' wages, which is money that has already been taxed at the corporate level).

To form a sole proprietorship, very little legal work is needed. Most states require you file a "Doing Business As" or *fictitious name (DBA)* to be able to do business under a different name (your company name). We will discuss DBA's later in this chapter.

Like a sole proprietorship, a **partnership** maintains the benefits, liabilities, income, and obligation in the hands of the owners – it is a type of FTE. The difference is that in a partnership there's more than one owner.

Partnerships can be in equal distribution (like 50/50) or the ownership can be disproportionate (50/30/20). With a partnership, the legal liabilities fall to the owners equally, despite the level of distribution of ownership. For example, a lawsuit or settlement against the partners will cost all partners the same amount – even if one partner owns 50%, another owns 30%, and another owns 20%. Additionally, anything one partner does reflects on the whole partnership, not on the individual.

Professional offices like lawyer firms and doctor groups often fall into partnerships, as do musical ensembles and some sales teams.

Forming a partnership is very similar to a sole proprietorship. You'll most likely need a DBA and you'll definitely need a partnership agreement. This is a legal document that outlines the responsibilities and scope of obligation of each partner.

Joint ventures are a type of partnership that forms for a specific purpose and for a limited time. For example, two authors cowriting a book or a team of people working on a video game design can form a joint venture. On paper these are still listed as partnerships, but the partnership will be dissolved once the goal is accomplished.

Limited partnerships (LP) are also like standard partnerships, but with one primary difference: One partner assumes the liabilities and obligations of the company and the other partners, known as limited partners, assume no or limited liability. Limited partners are usually not involved in the daily operational decisions of the business, thus acting more like employees in that respect.

A **limited liability company (LLC)** is also a type of FTE, but it provides the liability limitations that a corporation offers. In other words, although it is not an independent entity in the eyes of the law like a corporation, the individual owner(s) – sole proprietor or partners – would not be responsible for liabilities and obligations, but they would receive income directly like a sole proprietorship or partnership.

Because LLC's are not independent entities, taxes are generally filed on an individual's tax return – although there some states allow LLC's to file taxes as corporations.

To form an LP or LLC you'll need a DBA in most states as well as a partnership agreement (LP) or *articles of organization* (LLC); you'll also need an Employer Identification Number (EIN), which is obtained from the Federal Government.

A **corporation** is a separate entity in the eyes of the law. It has an EIN that acts like a social security number. It also has its own liabilities and obligations separate from any of the employees, owners, or investors.

For tax purposes, a corporation stands separate from the individuals involved in it – which is good from a liability standpoint, but it opens the door for double taxation as mentioned earlier in this chapter. Double taxation is where the corporation is taxed on earnings and then the employees (including the President, CEO, etc.) are taxed on their income – money that was already taxed at the corporate level.

To form a corporation you'll need a DBA, Articles of Incorporation, *EIN* (***Employer Identification Number*** – it's like a social security number for businesses), and licenses and permits, which vary by state.

You can file for an EIN here:
https://www.irs.gov/businesses/small-businesses-self-employed/employer-id-numbers

A **Not-for-Profit Corporation** is a tax-exempt organization, usually a charity. Known in the business world as a 501(c)(3), certain criteria must be met and maintained for it to keep its tax-exempt status. To obtain a license as a not-for-profit corporation, the organization must file IRS Form 1023, which can be obtained here: https://www.irs.gov/pub/irs-pdf/f1023.pdf

The requirements for filing a *DBA* vary by state (as of this writing, 13 states don't require it) but you should do it anyway. A DBA will allow you to do business under a different name than your own, even if you are the only employee of the company. Having a DBA will give you a sense of having a company separate from yourself and can boost your confidence when doing business.

DBA's are not complicated, but they may require some explanation. Let's say you have a partnership with Jenny Sue and Bobbi Lynn, which happens to be your musical group, *Roxy and the Frogettes*. Your

Partnership may be an LP called Crisan, Sue, and Lynn, LP. *Roxy and the Frogettes* would be your DBA.

With a corporation, things can get tricky – especially if you franchise your brand. Let's use Subway Restaurants as an example. The sandwich maker is officially listed with the government as a corporation called *Doctor's Associates*. This is because Fred DeLuca, a college student, asked family friend and doctor Peter Buck for the initial capital to fund his business venture. Subway is simply the brand owned by *Doctor's Associates*. If you were to purchase a Subway franchise, then your company may be called *Good Food, LLC* and have a DBA of "Subway" in Fort Lauderdale, Florida. So *Good Food, LLC* and *Doctor's Associates* have gone into a business agreement where you make the decisions for your franchise (this would be a type of partnership) and your DBA happens to be the same as the brand owned by *Doctor's Associates*. Sounds complicated, but it isn't, right?

Another thing you need to keep in mind is that if you run a retail outfit then you will most likely need to collect sales tax on behalf of your state (there are a few states where there is no sales tax, but this is the exception). Filing for a license to collect sales tax varies by state, but it is something you will surely want to get because it allows you to purchase products at wholesale price without having to pay sales tax on them.

*   *   *

Copyrights are governmental protections for creative works. Art, pictures, drawings, written works, music, and videos are all automatically protected by copyright in the United States as soon as they are created. However, it is very difficult to enforce a copyright for a work that you have not registered with the government. Copyrights are denoted with a ©. To register, go to: https://www.copyright.gov/registration/

You may have heard of the *"poor person's copyright"*, in which you would mail a sealed copy of the work to yourself and never open it unless you have to go to court. *Don't ever do this.* Filing for a copyright is inexpensive. Currently it costs about $35 for each work – music can be filed as a collection of 10-12 songs under a single filing. Short stories can be filed together as one work. Don't be cheap with this – registering grants you a legal protection that does not cost much and could save you a lot of grief in the future. A "poor person's copyright" is extremely difficult to defend in court.

Trademarks are a legal protection of brand items. Slogans, logos, brands, and company names can all be protected by trademarks; and they can be *registered* and *non-registered*. A registered trademark – usually denoted with an ® - is one that has been submitted to the U.S.. Patent and Trademark Office (USPTO) and has been granted a Trademark for Federal protection. A non-registered trademark – denoted with a ™ – has not been submitted or accepted by the USPTO. In other words, an unregistered trademark has federal protection but it is not registered with the government, so like with a "poor person's copyright" enforcing your protection would be very difficult.

Service Marks are like trademarks, but they are for brands that are not tangible – they are for services. For example, services like beauty salons, UPS or FedEx, Uber and Lyft, and HomeAgain Pet Tracking services can all have Service Marks. Registered and non-registered Service Marks both use the same symbol – the simple ^{SM} – to indicate that the brand is protected.

Filing a Trademark or Service Mark can cost upwards of $800 and can take about 7 months to a year if you do it yourself, but it requires a thorough search on the USPTO database of registered marks to ensure the mark does not already exist. If you file for a Trademark or Service Mark and there is already an identical registered mark that exists, you will lose your filing fee, as well as your protections.

This is why many business owners choose to hire an attorney who specializes in brand protection to handle the search and the filing. Such an attorney can cost your business up to ten times more to file than doing it yourself would and can take significantly more time, but it can be worth it if you are not confident in your ability to perform a thorough enough search. If you choose to do it yourself, though, you can go to www.uspto.gov to file.

Patents are protections for inventions. Once you have a design or prototype you should file for a patent. Like with Trademarks, a search for an existing patent is required prior to filing because the process for application takes about two years and, if not approved, you will lose your application fee - although there is an appeals process.

Patents will cost you a minimum of $4,000 once all is said and done, with no maximum. The fees vary depending on what is needed during your application process. For a list of fees and to file a patent yourself, you can go to: https://www.uspto.gov/learning-and-resources/fees-and-payment/uspto-fee-schedule.

To denote a patent, the patent registration number is listed next to the words "U.S. Patent #" or "U.S. Patent No." in an inconspicuous area of the product.

A ***Patent Pending*** status is similar to the ™ symbol for a Trademark – it provides no real protection because it only indicates that a patent has been applied for but has not yet been granted. Patents Pending are denoted with the words "Patent Pending" somewhere on the product.

Other protections afforded to your business come in the form of ***contracts***. Whether it's with customers, distributors, suppliers, or whatever, contracts are your ammunition to protect yourself in case something goes awry. Don't be scared to ask people you do business with to sign a contract. Trust is great, but being able to legally enforce obligations is priceless.

If you find a that person or other entity (business, etc.) is violating your rights, you need to enforce your protections – nobody else will do it for you. And the longer you wait, the harder it becomes to correct the problem.

The first step in protecting yourself is with a "***cease-and-desist***" order. This is a letter that is usually drafted by an attorney that tells the other party that they are infringing on your rights and they need to stop immediately or there will be further legal action; usually a C&D letter is enough to get the other party to stop doing what they're doing.

If, however, they do not stop within a reasonable amount of time, you will need to move to the next step – a lawsuit. It is not expensive to file a lawsuit. Or rather, lawsuits. An infringement of a trade/service mark, copyright, or patent can be brought to criminal court – yes, all of these would be Federal crimes – in which the infringer can do prison time depending on the severity of the infringement. You can also file in civil court for damages. In either case, most attorneys will not charge you unless you win the case, but even those that charge you up front will usually only charge a consultation fee (usually around $75) and the filing fee, which is about $400. Knowing this, you have no reason not to take the steps to protect yourself.

One final thought: when negotiating with investors things can get a bit muddy and convoluted. Have an attorney present during negotiations and don't let your investors' attorneys draft the term sheets or contracts. You are the business owner, so you have a lot to lose – keep the control in your hands.

The long and short of it:
- Decide what type of company works best for you: sole proprietorship, partnership, limited partnership, joint venture, limited liability company, corporation, and not-for-profit corporation
- File all of your legal paperwork to make it official: DBA, EIN, Partnership Agreement, Articles of Organization, Articles of Incorporation, and any other requirements needed in your state
- Corporations can be tax exempt. You will need to file IRS Form 1023 to obtain tax exempt status
- Collect taxes in your state if required, and get a license to do so – this will also give you tax exempt status when purchasing items wholesale
- Protect your products and services with Copyrights, Trademarks, Service Marks, Patents, and contracts as needed – and hire an attorney to file them if you are not confident in your ability to do it properly
- Enforce all of your legal protections and contractual obligations – don't hesitate to send out cease-and-desist orders, and don't hesitate to file lawsuits
- Don't let your investors' attorneys draft the term sheets or contracts

Protect Your Brand

"Brand yourself before others brand you."
-Unknown

A major goal of running a successful business is making that business stand out from the competition. Early on in the life of your company you'll need to figure out what type of message you want to convey – known as your brand - to your customers and potential customers, and how you will market that brand.

First, there is the consideration of your company name, slogan, and logo. A lot of thought and effort should go into creating each of these, because just like with anything that has to do with your business, failing to put the work in can prove disastrous.

There was a man named Greg that I was consulting locally through my company Fluharty and Johnson who wanted to open a toy and collectibles company in South Florida. After reviewing his business plan and other factors, we discussed his ideas for a company name. He told me he had "the one" and didn't need a list. When I asked him what name he had in mind, he revealed that he wanted to call it *Yesterday's Toys*.

At first glance this appears to be a great name that conveys the nostalgia of collectibles – but to me this just said, "these are the toys that nobody wanted and went out of fashion last year." This is not the message you want to convey for a modern toy store nor for a cool collectibles store.

But if *Yesterday's Toys* is bad, imagine if the sign for a clothing store called Kids Exchange had to be compressed just a bit to fit on the side of a building. The store would be receiving an entirely different clientele than they were expecting.

Another example is Optical store "For Eyes", which is a popular company where people can get glasses and lenses at reasonable prices. However, in the 1970's and 1980's, "four eyes" was a derogatory term for people with eyeglasses. The name of the company was a play on this as a way to celebrate people with glasses, but for me as a kid, this was a company I didn't want to give my money to – I'd heard the term enough at school from bullies.

Car maker Toyota had a marketing campaign with a slogan in 2016 that said, "We build owners." This is a very good slogan, especially for a car company. However, in their marketing materials the "d" and the "o" were so close that it looked like the slogan was "We build downers." This is not a message you want to convey to potential customers for the second largest investment in their life.

A good slogan can make your company a household name or it can ruin you. If you don't take time to perfect one and have a focus group assess it, you can end up with something disastrous in hand.

Your logo should also be simple and elegant and should clearly convey your message to a casual viewer. Think of logos for companies like Intel, Google, Apple, McDonald's, Amazon, and even Morton's salt. Successful logos are simple and effective, and don't overwhelm the viewer.

It's very easy to mess up a logo – not only with overwhelming details or that are hard to read like clothier Stussy or those of many custom car clubs and death metal bands (do an online search so you can see some examples), but also those that inadvertently offend.

American Pediatric Center, Locum, and the Catholic Archdiocesan Youth Commission (especially after recent scandals with the Catholic church) – these have all made errors with their logos that make them the brunt of many jokes. I encourage you to look these and the ones from prior paragraphs up online so you can get an idea of what I'm talking about. Those who say no publicity is bad publicity are completely wrong.

Also keep in mind that your logo and company name may not be yours forever – so make sure that the ones you choose are ones you are willing to part with. Remember Wally Amos and his "Famous Amos" brand; he no longer has any rights to that name.

*   *   *

Once you have gained some traction and your logo starts to become a household name, you can begin licensing it for different ventures. **Licensing** is allowing the use of your name, logo, or slogan by other companies in exchange for a fee. Many companies have "Officially Licensed" merchandise like t-shirts and stickers that help them bring in some additional income through the licensing agreements. Ford, Coca-Cola, Nasa, Marvel and DC Comics and many other organizations capitalize on the licensing market, and you can find t-shirts, cellphone cases, toys, and more with the branding of each of these organizations.

Be careful, however, of who you allow to utilize your brand and for what purpose. Allowing the wrong company to utilize your brand could make it look like your company endorses that specific item or action – or vice versa. For example, if you make ant and roach killer spray, you don't want your brand to end up on toys or children's t-shirts.

There are other forms of licensing – namely ***exclusive licensing***. This type of license allows exclusive use of the brand to the holder of the license. This is what happened to Marvel Comics Group when they almost went bankrupt in the late 1990's and early 2000's. In a desperate bid to keep afloat, the company began issuing exclusive licenses to movie studios and theme parks – so when the superhero movie craze of the 2010's hit, Marvel's characters were owned by three different studios and could never exist in the same cinematic universe. Some characters were owned by Fox, some by Sony, and some were owned by Marvel Studios proper (Disney). Purchasing the rights back has been a long and expensive process.

Additionally, Marvel superheroes were licensed out to Universal Studios theme parks, and now that Disney owns Marvel Comics Group, they still can't open a

Marvel heroes theme park because of this exclusive agreement.

As a lesson, if you issue an exclusive license, try to put a time limit on it.

*   *   *

Many organizations attract diehard fans who want to live and breathe the brand and want to show off their love for it. *Embrace these people!* Psychopathic Records attracts fans the company calls "Juggalos", who are given benefits like exclusive meet-and-greets, merchandise, and early access to show tickets just for being fans of their musical groups; there are Volkswagen beetle car clubs in which owners of the quirky model meet a few times a month to display their cars and have cookouts; and there are fans of the Monopoly board game who have started websites and who host playthroughs with other superfans regularly.

If your company has a fan club, embrace it; provide incentives to these people, because these are the people who will spread word about your company and do your marketing for you for free, and that's worth more than you could possibly imagine.

*   *   *

There are times when you will run into another company that has a company name, logo, or slogan that is very similar to yours. If you've read the *Legalease* chapter then you know that you need to protect every aspect of your business with copyrights, trademarks, and patents. If you've acquired these, then it is necessary that you issue (through your attorney if possible) a **cease and desist** letter to warn that business that they are infringing on your protected rights (copyright/trademark/service mark/patent). Failure to immediately rectify the situation should result in your suing that company for damages.

You cannot afford to feel bad for the owners of that company, even if it is a mom and pop business – they should have done their homework and built their business the correct way from the start. If they continue doing business in a way that could confuse customers and have them think it is your business, then it could end up costing *you*.

Imagine the owner of that business insults customers or does something bad that lands him on the local news; anyone who is insulted by him or who sees the news report will associate this behavior with your company. This is something that could cause irreparable damage, so nip it in the bud as quickly as you can.

*   *   *

Sometimes the negative publicity is not the result of some imposter – sometimes your own business falls into a dark place after some scandal is uncovered or some reporter writes an article or editorial that paints you in a negative light.

If this happens, don't lash out; deny it if it's a complete fabrication, but be humble. If it's not a fabrication, don't lie – better to admit it early and move forward with damage control than to deny it and drag out the narrative. As Thomas Jefferson once said, "If you have to eat crow, eat it while it's young and tender." If you lie and deny, everyone will know about it anyway and it'll just make things worse.

In 2010 British Petroleum had a highly publicized oil spill in the Gulf of Mexico. CEO Tony Hayward appeared on television and famously blamed the owner of the oil rig, American company Transocean. He said, "This was not our accident… this was not our drilling rig… this was Transocean's rig. Their systems. Their people. Their equipment."

The problem with this type of response is that the public does not distinguish between Transocean and BP. Transocean's rig was leased by BP, and to the casual observer, that made it BP's rig. The backlash against BP was massive. People refused to purchase gas at their gas stations. Owners of BP franchises pleaded with the public to be conscious of the fact that their stations were not corporate owned. But again, the normal layman only sees BP on the sign and makes the association.

This is like when you call customer service at a company and the agent tells you, "That's not my department." To the customer, your company is a single entity. Telling them that different departments handle different aspects of the account does nothing to aid the customer and it does nothing but frustrate and upset them.

If you find yourself in a crisis like the ones above, don't doubt for a minute that your competition will seize such an opportunity to pounce. Your brand should stand apart regardless of any temporary issues, and after you recover, keep pushing forward and continue to create competitive advantages (see chapter *Leverage Your Advantage*).

*   *   *

Terminating employees is sometimes necessary to save face with customers and suppliers. If an employee, who is a representative of your company, is not working out, end the relationship for the sake of your brand. The same thing goes for suppliers who are rude to your customers or who have issues that can lead to negative publicity – like Transocean and BP, your suppliers and other business partners work for you and are thus viewed as part of your business. If the relationship is not working out, end it as soon as possible.

*   *   *

One final note about your brand. There are brands that become such household names that the company loses ownership of their trademark in what's called a **_proprietary eponym_** or **_genericized trademark_**.

You probably use many of these words on a daily basis and are aware that they're brands, but some may be surprising to you. Following is a short list of brands that have become proprietary eponyms:

Frisbee, Q-Tip, Band-Aid, Rubix Cube, Microchip, Styrofoam, Xerox (although they have fought very hard to regain their brand and have mostly succeeded, with the exception of some older folks who still refer to photocopying as "making a Xerox"), Aspirin, Tylenol, Escalator, Dry Ice, Zipper, Coke, Walkie Talkie, Dumpster, Trampoline, Laundromat, Videotape, Yo-Yo, and Jacuzzi.

Realize that once you lose your trademark, it is very difficult to reclaim it. Sure, it's great to have everyone call certain goods or services by your brand name, but they will even be calling your competitors' goods and services by your brand name – which means you have now become a commodity and can no longer compete on quality – which means you can only compete on price. We discuss this further in the chapter on becoming a low-cost provider later in the book.

Your brand:
- Your company name, slogan, and logo need to convey your core message to your customers
- Be careful not to inadvertently have a company name or slogan that offends people or puts a negative light on your company
- Your company name, logo, and slogan may not be yours forever
- You can make extra money licensing your brand
- Be mindful of who you provide an official license to
- Exclusive licenses can cause you trouble in the future – if you issue one, put a time limit if you can
- Protect your brand – don't hesitate to issue a *cease and desist* letter if your brand is being exploited
- Negative publicity can destroy your business – so be humble and do damage control as soon as possible
- Don't shift blame on another company or another department – take ownership of the problem Employees who are not properly representing your company need to be removed quickly
- Business partners work for you and are therefore just like employees in the eyes of the customer
- Keep your brand from becoming a proprietary eponym

Leverage Your Advantage

"If you don't have a competitive advantage, don't compete."
— Jack Welch

Imagine that all car makes and models cost the same. What would make you pick one over the other? Would it be the size, the quality of the workmanship, the place of manufacture, the model name? Seriously think about this and try to come up with three models from any make that you would choose in this scenario and list your reasons why. Without a price comparison it becomes a bit more difficult in a way, but it also becomes a bit easier to come to a decision. This is because certain vehicles have a competitive advantage – one that transcends price - over other vehicles.

A competitive advantage is real, palpable – it is something all your customers can agree to be true.

It should also be something that can't be undone or copied too easily by your competition. Likewise, try to find what advantages your competitors have over you so you can thwart them or at least have a rebuttal when their sales staff brings it up to your customers.

Back in 2005 when cellphones operated on a 3G platform, AT&T ran a campaign that said, "We have more towers than Verizon or Sprint." This was actually true; but the reason they had more towers was not clearly related to customers. See, 3G technology was in reality an umbrella term that included 3G GSM and 3G CDMA technologies. To a casual user, there was no difference. However, there were several major differences.

GSM was the "**G**lobal **S**tandard for **M**obile Communication" – a technology that utilized sim cards to guide the device to find a signal from a GSM tower. CDMA, on the other hand, was an advanced technology developed by the US military for secure communication. It was more secure than GSM and didn't use sim cards; the device itself had a built-in communication band that connected it to 3G CDMA towers. And each CDMA tower could handle five (5) times the number of calls that a GSM tower could. So yes, AT&T had more towers, but it was because they *had to have more towers* just to compete. Verizon and Sprint never rebutted AT&T's claims, and AT&T became one of the top two and has remained there for many years.

One place where the competition did rebut AT&T was in Rollover Minutes. In those days, cellular phone calling plans were sold by bundles of minutes. Any minutes that remained unused by the end of the month were discarded; any minutes over the allotted amount were charged at a premium. AT&T, however, came up with a great way to set themselves apart from the competition: Rollover Minutes.

The concept of Rollover Minutes was that any unused minutes on a given month carried over to the following month, so that if you had overages, rather than charging you money, AT&T would deduct the applicable number of minutes that had "rolled over". Verizon and Sprint, however, used this to their advantage. The two companies began to train their staff to rebut any customer that mentioned Rollover Minutes by saying, "If you are rolling minutes over, then you're on the wrong plan." It worked in most cases, but the two companies failed to use this line in any of their marketing, which would have carried the message a lot further.

Another missed opportunity came when the first iPhone was released. At the time, almost every phone was capable of sending Multimedia Messaging Service (MMS) messages and operated on the 3G network. The first iPhone, however, was not capable of MMS and it operated on the Edge network (a 2G network) as opposed to 3G. Despite this, Apple (the manufacturer of the iPhone) promoted the device as a game changer and a true innovation that was ahead of its time.

The first iPhone did have some new features not seen on any other device prior; namely, it had an accelerometer that allowed it to know if it was being held upright or sideways. It was the first phone to use a glass screen, which make it look very sleek; and it also helped to introduce the concept of an app store where a user could easily find several different programs to install on the phone. But the device was far from a game-changer.

The competition failed to capitalize on these weaknesses, and the iPhone sold an unprecedented number of units just on its first day. Still today, Apple products are very restricted: all apps must be purchased through their app store; music on the device must be transferred through iTunes; the home and lock screens can't be customized with the user's own personal photo or with themes; and you can't install apps like Swipe, Trigger, Scheduler, Automatic Call Recorder, or RFC tag programmers like TagWriter.

Other Apple devices have had similar issues: the first Apple Watch was not water resistant and it could not work away from the iPhone it was linked to. It was a dependent piece of technology. The device also had to be used exclusively with an iPhone, which is not a problem for Apple enthusiasts, but for a casual user it can be a problem.

Apple's competition needs to capitalize on their advantages over Apple to boost their own sales – but they are failing to do so. As a business owner, you need to not only have Competitive Advantages (CA's) of your own, you need to know your competitor's advantages and weaknesses and take advantage of or exploit them. Highlight the areas where you are stronger or appear stronger.

But a word of warning: do not lie. People familiar with the industry knew AT&T was trying to deceive the public – and this really didn't look good for them. People will know when you lie, and if you think that you can get away with it, you may very well do so – but at the very least your competition will know you are lying and they can exploit this at any time.

Also, keep in mind that as your business grows so does the number of competitors you will have. And the more competitors you have, the more ruthless the narrative. You will be outed as a liar sooner than later.

You need your competitive advantages to remain ahead of the competition. As an example, take a look at what happened with Blockbuster Video. The movie rental giant had almost as many stores as McDonald's at its peak. The company was thriving and easily became a household name. Then a little company called Netflix came out and offered unlimited rentals for a flat monthly fee; you just had to create a want list online and they would send you dvd's via mail. The return mailing was free. And when you mailed a movie back, they mailed you the next one on your list. There were also no late fees, because you could keep the movie as long as you wanted.

Around the same time, another company called RedBox began placing kiosks at Walgreens pharmacies, Walmart superstores, and many other locations throughout the country. RedBox allowed you to rent a DVD or Blu-Ray disc for a low price and return it at any other RedBox kiosk for no additional fee.

Blockbuster began losing market share to these two new competitors very quickly, but they hesitated in their response. Months after Netflix appeared as a competitor, Blockbuster Video removed their late fees. A few months after that, they implemented a flat fee/unlimited rental program. And almost a year after RedBox appeared, Blockbuster began placing their own kiosks throughout the country. But the damage was done.

Blockbuster lost market share very quickly and the new competitive spaces – mail-order rentals and unlimited plans, kiosk rentals – were already established without them. They were a late entry into those spaces, and their days were numbered as a result; Blockbuster became a brand of the past. Not long after they introduced their new products Blockbuster Video went out of business. They simply failed to create and maintain competitive advantages, and they completely failed to overcome their competitors'.

Another example of a company failing to capitalize on its competitive advantage (or rather, letting their advantage lapse) and allowing the competitor to take over all the market share is MySpace.com. MySpace was one of the first social networks on the internet, and it was hugely popular. It allowed the user to fully customize their page with HTML programming, allowing imbedding of pictures, music and video. No other platform came close.

There was another social network at the time that was exclusive to college students – it was called *The Facebook* and it allowed the user to create a profile only if he had a college or university email address. The exclusivity made it seem safe and it also made people want to join just to see what it was about. The Facebook eventually got renamed to simply "Facebook" and slowly began to allow non-students to join.

As a social media platform, Facebook was inferior to MySpace in many ways. It did not have a messaging function, one could not fully customize pages (it didn't allow HTML programming code) nor embed media, and it was limited in many ways. However, the site started to gain traction once it opened up to anyone who wanted to create a profile, and quickly overcame the popular MySpace. Now MySpace is a music specialty social media site, with less than half the users that Facebook has. And all of this is because they failed to capitalize on their competitive advantages.

In her book, *Creating Competitive Advantage* (Currency/Doubleday, 2006), Jaynie L. Smith states that all of your business and strategic decisions should be founded in your competitive advantages. She also provides some excellent advice on how to build and exploit your advantages.

Creating a competitive advantage is not difficult, but it takes careful crafting. Your advantages must be specific and must convey to your customers what your company can do for them that would boost their business or improve their life that the competition can't do. For example, stating that "We get results" is terrible; and stating, "We make service our #1 priority" is abysmal – every company claims this.

Instead of those generalities, some examples of good competitive advantages would be: "All our chickens are free-range in ten acres of land"; or, "We use no hormones and our cows are all grass-fed"; or, "Our gasoline removes 75% of impurities – clean your engine while you drive"; or, "Bring your pet along! We love seeing your four-legged family members in our store."

When it comes to a product, remember the difference between features and benefits. Features are descriptors of your product or service. For example, "This television remote has 87 buttons and comes in 22 different colors."

Benefits are what the product or service can do for the customer. For example, "This television remote allows you to skip commercials"; or "This television remote is easy to program – just push one button and the remote does the rest!"

These benefits are your competitive advantages, so know them and make sure all your employees and customers know them, too. Don't feel ashamed to drill these advantages in until people are sick of hearing them – believe me, you can't push them enough.

Mrs. Smith also mentions that there are two types of Competitive Advantages: internal and external. Internal advantages are those that customers can't immediately see, such as a highly effective distribution network or sales staff that are also engineers.

External advantages are those that are immediately visible to the customer, such as an open platform on Android devices or lightweight materials on a shoe.

You need both types of advantages to succeed in business, but because internal advantages are not immediately visible to the general public, it takes significantly more effort to highlight those to customers.

Still, you need to make a serious effort to tout all of your advantages and educate customers in such a way that they are able to repeat and tout them along with you to others. Remember, your company will only be as successful as its competitive advantages over the competition – so make sure that these are clearly defined and exploited.

Advantage points:
- Competitive advantages allow you to transcend price
- CA's are real and palpable – and all your customers can agree that it is an advantage over the competition
- Build advantages that can't be easily copied
- Learn of your competitors' advantages and prepare a rebuttal against them
- The bigger your business, the more competition you'll have – you need CA's to help you stand out
- Don't lie
- Create advantages that are specific and convey a clear message

Communication

"The alternative to the Golden Rule is the Platinum Rule: Treat others the way they want to be treated."
-Dr. Tony Alessandra

They say communication is a two-way street; so, it comes as no surprise that the Bible-derived Golden Rule, to treat others as you'd like to be treated, is the primary rule of communication. And, although this is not how the original directive was phrased (in the Bible it tells people to "not treat others in a way you don't want to be treated"), both versions are still flawed when it comes to communication. After all, most of us have different expectations during interactions, and if all we do is simply force our own beliefs and expected actions on others we interact with, we are acting in an authoritative way which can turn off many of those with whom we wish to do business.

Dr. Tony Alessandra's Platinum Rule, quoted above, presents a very simple, yet overlooked, solution to the problems many people and companies have when communicating with others – particularly partners and customers. It would be amazing if everyone treated us how *we* wanted to be treated!

The first step to communicating effectively is understanding who you are and what you want to communicate. As the owner of an organization, everything you or any of your employees does or says is a representation of your company – this is even true after work hours for employees who are still in uniform. It is more true, however, for you as the owner. You will *always* be the face of the company.

Understand that communication is not just about actions and words, though. The way you dress or present yourself is also communicating something about your company to bystanders and onlookers.

That's why it's so important to always look your best – if you are a man, shave daily; men and women should look neat and their clothes should be pressed (or at least not wrinkled), and they should act professionally at all times. Avoid profanity and coarse language at all times, and watch what you say on your social media accounts – even your personal ones.

You also need to understand the person or persons you're communicating with and what their expectations are during any interaction. Only with this understanding can you get your message across. If you don't meet the expectations of the message receiver, then they will not pay any attention to the message.

For example, if the other person expects you to tell them about your product and instead you start spewing off about your company and your personal achievements, they will quickly walk away and look for the information on their own.

When interacting with people it is expected that you listen 75% of the time and speak only 25%. It's good to always keep this in mind because people like to talk about themselves and you need to be the ear that listens, because if it's *you* talking about yourself, then chances are the person isn't going to be interested. Think of a time you met someone for the first time and all they did was talk about themselves. It was probably very annoying. But if you both decide to just listen, don't think this would make for boring conversation; it won't. If both parties listen most of the time, this just means that the conversation will be more to the point.

Now, communication isn't only about talking. Your company communicates with customers and investors in many other ways; whether it's the color selection of a product (Henry Ford once famously said that people could have a Model T in any color as long as it was black), the packaging, your marketing, and more. Think very deeply about what you would like to communicate to your customers and make decisions based on that.

The other side of the coin is with your customers communicating with your company. Remember that 75% / 25% ratio? Make sure that remains true when the communication is between your company and your customers. Listen to your customers – they love to give their opinion on things.

Ways you could learn what people are saying or thinking is through social media, product reviews, surveys, focus groups, etc. But the best way to get customer feedback is to talk to them during your daily sales interactions. Ask customers what they're looking for – and then listen to what they say.

You are in business for your customers, after all; don't forget that. Keep an open ear and an open mind, because customers can present you with great insights on how you can improve your sales, service, product, marketing, employees, and interactions.

It is important to note, however, that the input from a single customer is not enough for you to make an informed decision for change. You'll need to hear the same thing from several customers before taking any serious action – but take every comment and all feedback seriously.

There was a great *Seinfeld* episode in which the title character and his friends went to a new Italian restaurant. The owner was Pakistani, so Seinfeld told him he should change the concept to a Pakistani restaurant. The man made the change but ended up ruined because none of the locals wanted to try Pakistani food. The episode was hilarious, but you don't want to make that kind of mistake based on the input of a single customer.

To avoid this, be clear in what you're trying to find out; an open-ended and open subject survey that lacks direction will lead you exactly there – nowhere fast. Have a reason or two for your survey so that the answers from all customers can help guide your decision-making.

So, instead of, "What can we do to improve?" you should ask, "What can we do to improve the taste of this milkshake? More vanilla? Less sugar? Larger portion?"

If you go into it with purpose, asking customers for their feedback on specific attributes of your product or business can be very productive and extremely insightful. It can also help make your business the best in its industry.

Application of communication:
- Have an understanding of the message you want to convey to others
- Your employees represent your company while in uniform
- You are *always* representing your company
- The way you dress and present yourself communicates a lot about you and your company
- Know the expectations of the person you're communicating with
- Listen 75% of the time, talk 25%
- Your company can communicate in other ways, such as color selection of your product, packaging, marketing, etc.
- Listen to customer feedback
- Feedback from a single customer should not guide your decision-making
- Have a specific reason for your survey: to find out if your drink is too sweet or needs more salt, rather than something vague like, "how can we improve the product?" ask "Was it too sweet?" or "Does it need more salt?"

Your Core Business

"Be what you are. This is the first step toward becoming better than you are."
-Julius Charles Hare

In the late 1950's and early 1960's there was a man named Joe Coulombe who owned a chain of convenience stores named Pronto Market. Coulombe had some stiff competition with 7-11 and other convenience stores that offered a bevvy of items their customers could easily obtain at all hours of the day or night. Disillusioned, Coulombe took some time off and traveled to the Caribbean to get his mind off things.

While there, Coulombe got inspiration to make his stores as easy as the Caribbean – so he trimmed down the number of SKU's in his stores to one of each (one brand of milk, cheese, etc.) and decided to carry items that were fresh and more difficult to find than items that were sold at 7-11 stores.

In 1968, he renamed the first store "Trader Joe's" and solidified the concept of an easy Caribbean feel and fresh, exotic food. This set him apart from 7-11 and launched his stores into a different space than the convenience store space that 7-11 was in.

Today Trader Joe's is owned by a German ***holding company*** that also owns Aldi food stores and boasts more than 470 Trader Joe's stores nationwide.

What Joe was able to accomplish after his trip to the Caribbean is change what his core business was all about. He was able to remove his company from its original market, which was convenience stores, and enter a new market that had little competition.

When he made this move, Joe also managed to redefine his company and stand out from his previous competitors. In addition, once he made the switch, Joe stuck to his guns and never wavered, making his brand a reliable, consistent source for what his customers wanted.

When you're just starting out as a new company, you need to focus on your core business. Do what you originally went into business to do and don't deviate from it. Wait until your company has been established in its core business before you try to grow beyond it. So, if your company makes basketballs, then stick to that before you move on to making clothing and baseball bats and catchers' mitts.

The reason for this is that you will spread yourself out too thin if you expand to other industries before establishing yourself in your original one.

In the example of Trader Joe's, Joe Coulombe knew he wanted to be in the food business, but he also knew that he didn't want to compete with giants like 7-11. What he did instead was change his core business. He entered the fresh food market space and found success. What he didn't do, however, was remain in the convenience space *and* also open a chain of fresh food markets. It's an important difference to keep in mind.

Virgin Airlines had some moderate success in the early 2000's before CEO Richard Branson decided to delve into space travel. The company suffered some losses and eventually got bought out by Alaska Airlines, and Branson branched out into other ventures such as Virgin Hyperloop One – a company dedicated to reducing transport time for goods and people through the use of hyperloop technology. Virgin's goals for space travel were eventually confined to a subsidiary of Virgin Group named Virgin Galactic, but it is undeniable that delving into space travel before Virgin Airlines was financially stable had a profound impact on these results.

Car manufacturer Tesla found success in its electric cars in recent years, but they are also looking into space travel in the near future - beginning with the recent SpaceX launch of a sportscar through into orbit. The company is still young, and CEO Elon Musk is ambitious in his endeavors, so it remains to be seen what kind of impact this type of venture would have on a company with very little market share in its industry.

In direct contrast, Danish toy manufacturer Lego Group realized that their standard building blocks were only appropriate for children over 5 years old because of a choking hazard for younger children. The company had been around for over 30 years when in 1969 they launched Duplo, which was their building blocks targeted at children younger than 6 years old. This not only opened their market to a new age group, it also allowed the indoctrination of children from a younger age into their products.

Coincidentally, Lego Group is the world's largest tire manufacturer – but they have never tried to make tires for full-size automobiles because the company understands that a horizontal move such as this would be risky and could prove fatal for their business. Instead, the company continues to focus on their standard products, Lego Building Blocks and Duplo Sets, and in recent years they have focused on animation. Their DC Heroes and Villains are popular with both adults and children, as are their Ninjago characters – so the company partnered with Warner Brothers Pictures to produce animated films and television series based on these characters.

Sadly for the Danish company, these animated features have underperformed at the box office, although the licensed merchandise remains popular. It was a calculated risk, but not one that was too successful for Lego Group.

One industry where the company has performed well is in its theme park ventures. These parks feature rides based on Lego sets and films and they also sell Lego Building Blocks and Duplo Sets at their souvenir shops.

It's important to note that these ventures have come almost 100 years after the company was started, and decades after it established itself as a household name. The lesson here is that you need to make sure that you can stand before you try to dance.

Take Coca-Cola, the soft drink manufacturer based in Atlanta, Georgia, for example. Over the years the company has made investments in several ***vertical ventures***: other soft drinks, water, orange juice, tea, and others.

The company owns strictly food brands (primarily beverages), but has tried its hand at other, horizontal ventures – most famously by purchasing Columbia Pictures film studios in the 1980's. After a couple of years of moderate success, the company sold the studio to Sony.

Since then, Coca-Cola has stuck to its core business and invests strictly in vertical ventures; they remain the best-selling soft drink in most countries and are one of the top five largest brands in the world.

Now, expansion is not the same as diversification. Blockbuster Video's failures were in its lack of diversification and vision – so they quickly stagnated and fell behind in their own industry. We will discuss diversification in a future chapter but remember that for any ***horizontal endeavors*** – those that are in a different industry or market than the one your company was originally a part of – you should open a subsidiary company. Much like how Virgin has Virgin Galactic, Ford has Jaguar (regular and luxury), Honda has Acura, Nissan has Infinity, and Johnson & Johnson has a myriad collection of brands for each space they are in, your business, too, should differentiate its brands by sector.

Just because your brand has success in one industry does not guarantee it will have success in another; in fact, from historical examples, a brand that is established in one sector will not likely succeed in another under the same brand.

At the core:
- Identify your core business and decide if that is the space you want to compete in
- If you are ready to expand, stick to vertical ventures; that is, invest in ventures within your industry until you are solid in your core business
- Horizontal ventures (outside of your industry) are extremely risky, even for large, established companies; if they won't do it, you shouldn't either – at least not at first
- Diversification is for growth – don't confuse diversification with needless expansion
- Open subsidiary companies for horizontal endeavors

Daily Operation

"Small daily habits lead to long-term growth."
-Unknown

Although the Business Plan contains guidelines for your business's operational requirements, it does not get too specific in regards to the daily operation of your business. Your business needs an ***operations manual*** to dictate what is required each and every day you operate.

Your operations manual needs to contain instructions for employees to follow daily in case you're not there to supervise. It also serves as a guidebook for managers that you hire and helps to do two other things: 1. It helps to guide your employees and puts all of your expectations in writing so that there is no doubt as to what is expected of them, and 2. It keeps you from micromanaging your employees and from having to repeat every day what it is you want your employees to do. The operations manual should also include sections that mirror the employee manuals; you should have an employee manual for each position, detailing each job description and its duties.

One of the main things that your operations manual should include (especially if you're in retail) is the opening and closing procedures. In this section you should detail the steps employees should take during opening and closing a store, office, warehouse, or whatever. It should also include what the managerial duties are during this time of day.

The subject of security should also be discussed in great detail in your operations manual. This section should discuss security alarms, cash register/ till counts, cash denominational set-up (how many of each bill and coin), takedown, storage, as well as the safe – everything from changing combination codes, emptying the safe, and what expectations you have regarding door locks.

Things like what to do in an emergency situation (disaster, robbery, medical emergency), procedures for contacting the authorities, safe lock-out, "dropping" cash overages from registers into a lockbox throughout the day, and other security issues should all be discussed in your operations manual.

Remember that if you're not going to use an armed security deposit service for your bank deposits, you need to have a randomized time and date for your deposits to avoid being targeted by thieves (both internal and external). Also, never carry your deposits in a bank bag, cash box, or anything else that can be easily identified as a cash deposit.

Part of your security also involves your computers – so make sure you have procedures for computer back-up and maintenance in your manual. Identify possible security risks and what to do in case of a breach. If your business depends on computers, list procedures in case the power goes out or your computers are compromised or disabled so a failure doesn't stop you from operating.

Additionally, cleaning should be discussed, along with who bears the responsibility to clean every day and whether the cleaning should be done before the day begins, at the end of the day, or both.

The manual should also have a section that defines the accounting method: the software used, database maintenance, and who enters the data and how often. In addition to software, this section should also outline the keeping of receipts; from purchase receipts and purchase orders to sales receipt copies, summaries, and reports. There needs to be direction on how and where to store these, as well as guidelines on digitizing them.

Inventory is extremely important to a commodity (non-service) business and especially to retail and foodservice. Explain to employees how often inventory should be taken and how to keep track of it (like which software to use). For restaurants, you need to plan on how to store and label the food, and how long each type of food item should be stored before it's thrown out.

If you're in retail, have a standard order or purchase order format printed and available for your employees; maybe include a copy in the manual that a manager can simply photocopy. If you are an office or warehouse, have back-ups and procedures for those back-ups; maybe tablets that connect to the internet wirelessly can be used temporarily in place of desktops to continue running the business in a time of crisis.

Timekeeping is also a concern for employees, especially in case of a blackout. Explain in your manual how time records are kept and how payroll is administered. If time logs are digitized (on the computer) then list alternative ways for time records to be kept temporarily and delineate the procedures for entering and approving that time once power comes back on. Dictate who would be responsible for this duty.

And while we're on the topic of timesheets, you need to ensure that you include a section that outlines the procedures for Human Resources and Benefits.

When it comes to Human Resources (HR) your company needs to utilize resources to make employees feel like they're a valuable asset of your company. In fact, they may be the most valuable asset. So have a plan and procedure that would let employees know who to go to if they have a concern or even suggestions for your business to improve. Employees need to know that there is an ear they could turn to with their issue without fear of repercussion. You never know, your employees might have some concerns about a manager or other employee that could save you from a scandal, or they may have a suggestion that explodes into the next big thing.

Employees also need to know where to go with questions about their benefits. Even if you don't think you offer benefits to your employees, you do. Whether it's employee discounts on products you sell, paid time off, holiday pay, emergency medical leave, worker's compensation, or others they can all be listed under benefits and 99% of businesses offer at least two or three of these to their employees.

*   *   *

The old adage that says that "the customer is always right" is more than just something you should be regurgitating daily; it is a mantra that you should be living as you go about your daily business. When I was consulting, I had a client who owned a beauty salon. She had ordered an inordinate quantity of a new shampoo that had some kind of rare seaweed extract or whatever, so it was very expensive. Andrea had ordered a bunch of bottles to get a bulk discount and be able to maximize her profits.

What Andrea decided to do to try and push sales of this shampoo was to provide samples to customers who used her salon services. One day, while I was at her salon reviewing some of her inventory, a customer had just finished getting her hair dyed and she was on her way to wash her hair. Andrea told her about the sample and gave the bottle to the customer. Several minutes later, the customer emerged dressed and ready to go, but she didn't give the bottle of shampoo back to Andrea. As a result, Andrea snapped at the customer and accused her of trying to steal the entire bottle!

I told Andrea to go to the back for a moment and I apologized to the customer. After she told me she misunderstood that the sample was just a single use from the big bottle, I told her that I understood and was sorry. I let her keep the entire bottle, and when she left I explained to Andrea that if she wanted to stay in business past a year, she had to give customers the benefit of the doubt – especially when she herself was vague about the samples.

I don't know if the customer ever came back, but I know that if it was me, I wouldn't. To have the owner or even an employee snap at you because they weren't clear with instructions on something is completely unacceptable.

In Hollywood, Florida there's a very large hotel and casino in which there is a restaurant called the Blue Plate. My brother and I at the time had just written *The Re-evolution Project* and were doing consulting for shy men to learn social skills. We took a client out to the casino (which has a lot of clubs and stores where he could practice his social skills) and spent several hours there. At about midnight, we decided to get a bite to eat; we sat down at the Blue plate and ordered burgers and sodas.

The sodas came out right away, but the burgers took a very long time. Almost 40 minutes passed, and we decided it was taking too long – so we told our waitress to just close out our check, cancel the burgers, and we'd pay for what we consumed. She refused and called the manager, who in turn called the Seminole Police. The police had us pay for our sodas (which is what we were trying to do anyway) and escorted us out with our client and issued us all a trespass warning.

This is not how to treat customers. The right thing to do here was for the manager to apologize and close out our check, period. I even told him that, had this been my elderly parents, I was sure he would have acted differently. He knew I was right, but became indignant. We weren't looking for anything for free, we just wanted to leave, and yet he escalated it to the point where the police embarrassed three customers and made them feel like criminals.

Don't become this business; treat all customers the same way. Avoid accusing customers of wrongdoing when it was your business that made the mistake; remember that perception is reality.

A powerful policy you can have in any business is to empower your employees to do the right thing without having to consult a manager; your customers will keep coming back. Nothing is more refreshing than going to a place of business where the employees are able to make decisions without having to ask their boss for permission. It shows you trust your employees and that you believe in your business.

And this brings us to the quote at the beginning of the chapter: always remember the Platinum Rule: treat people how they want to be treated – not just how *you* want to be treated or how you think *they* want to be treated. Talk to your customers and find out what they want, then do it *their* way.

*   *   *

Many business owners, when speaking about the success of their business, will discuss how much money they've made in the last year. It is important, however, to know the difference between revenue and profit. **Revenue** is the total amount of money your business brings in. This is basically your total sales before any costs are factored in. **Profits** are the totals monies received after costs are factored in. So a company that had $1.1m in sales last year could still lose money if their costs are $1.3m.

Once you understand the difference, you need to ensure that every single day your aim is to bring in a profit. That's the goal of running a business – after all, if you're not profitable, then you're losing money. And if you're losing money, then your business becomes like that child who celebrates his 21st birthday and is still living at home, not working, and taking an allowance.

This is not to say that revenue is a bad statistic, though. There are times when your business just needs to pay the bills and increasing your revenue – even if not exactly profitable – is what will keep you afloat. Some retail companies like Walgreens have items that they make no money on or actually lose money on; the purpose of these products is to up revenue and get people in the door. These are called **doorbuster deals** or just doorbusters.

The purpose of doorbusters is to get the customer in the door and while in the store, entice the customer to purchase other, more profitable items. You will notice that the doorbuster items are never near the entrance or exit – they are usually at the back of the store so that the customer has to pass many other departments or sections before arriving at their target. If you run a retail establishment and have doorbusters, you need to do this.

Even if your store is strictly online, there are ways you can implement these strategies on a website. For example, you can list your doorbuster deal at the bottom of a page or have pop-ups offering your more profitable items whenever someone places the doorbuster deal in their shopping cart. There are many other ways you can maximize profits and revenue online, and I recommend you get a book on online sales to help you with this.

If you're in retail, you can implement some basic marketing strategies in your daily operation to ensure you're profitable every day. You should buy a book on sales and marketing and make a list of relevant tactics that will help you increase revenue and profits, but here is another tactic that works well, just like doorbusters.

There was a study done years ago that revealed a very interesting trait of consumer behavior. Moviegoers at a movie theater were given two options for concessions: a large popcorn for $7 or a small popcorn for $3. Almost all of the moviegoers selected the small popcorn because they didn't want to spend $7. The next group of moviegoers were given three options: $3 for a small, $6.50 for a medium, and $7 for a large popcorn. In this case, almost all of the patrons elected to purchase the $7 large popcorn because they saw it as the best deal.

This effect is formally known as asymmetrically dominated choice, or more commonly known as the ***decoy effect***. The psychology of it all gets very detailed and there are many theories that surround this phenomenon, but all you need to know is that it works and can help you to maximize sales. This can be used even with services; for example, if you run a pool cleaning service, you can offer a single cleaning for $35, three cleanings for $85, or four cleanings for $100.

This decoy effect can also be used for items you sell online.

Don't think that you'll make less by selling the largest quantity at such a discount. Remember that the mid-level price is a decoy, and chances are very low that you'll ever sell that. The low price is also a decoy (although more people will take you up on that over the mid-level price), but the price should be an inflated price regardless. Consider it a bonus if someone selects that option. Your goal is to sell the most expensive one to maximize revenue while still making a profit. Plus, based on the principle of ***economies of scale***, the more expensive one should actually cost you less than the least expensive one on a per-unit ratio due to increased savings as production increases.

Imagine a person making a shirt, then a pair of pants, then a pair of shoes. Now imagine instead three people working, each one specializing in one thing. One makes three shirts, the other makes three pants, and the other makes three pairs of shoes. In this second example, the skill set gained by these specialized workers after each item is made allows each subsequent item to be made quicker and more efficiently.

The same rule applies to a service. Sticking with the pool maintenance example from earlier, imagine the employee has to find the address, figure out the best way to service a particular pool, etc. If he has to do three pools individually, it may take him a long time on each one. But now imagine he does the same pool three times; each time he does the pool he gets faster and more efficient in both finding the address and servicing that particular pool. This is why selling a package actually doesn't make you less money, but rather more money.

Now, there is such a thing as the *law of diminishing returns*, which states that your savings reach a peak after a certain point and then each unit produced after that costs you more and more - until you're actually losing money with each unit you manufacture or each service you provide.

With the pool example, imagine the employee has to go to the same pool twice per day, every day. The work will become tedious and monotonous, and cleaning the pool is in reality wasting the employee's energy and resources that could be better utilized elsewhere. Keep all of this in mind when pricing your products and services, and when creating packages or bundles for customers.

A similar tactic to the bundle that you can use is the *twofer* – where for example you have "one for $79 or two for $100." This maximizes revenue by enticing customers to purchase the more expensive two-set because they see it as a deal over buying just one. A customer who was planning on buying only one and spending $79 at your place of business would now be spending $100 instead.

Payless Shoe Source utilizes this technique. For each pair of shoes you purchase at full price, you can get a second pair of equal or lesser value for half price.

Needless to say, most customers take advantage of the deal because they don't want to miss out on getting a second pair for such a deep discount. Even if they don't need another pair of shoes, customers will shell out the money just because they see this as a savings, not as an expense. This is how the company has remained in business for decades, even through the Great Recession.

Another way you can up your revenue is with combos. Think of fast food restaurants like Wendy's or McDonald's. You can order items a la carte, but you save money as a customer if you order a combo that includes the entrée, a side, and a drink. The soft drinks cost these restaurants almost nothing, so most of the cost difference is buffed by that product. Find out within your industry what products are usually purchased together and build combos around these that also include additional products to maximize your revenue and profitability.

Finally, there is something most of us are familiar with, formally known as the ***left-digit effect***. This technique takes an item price and reduces it by one cent to make it end in .99. So, an item that should be priced at $30 is usually priced at $29.99 instead. The reason for this is most people only look at the numbers before the decimal, and don't mentally round up. The technique works very well, and now a new technique is gaining traction, especially with companies like Brandsmart USA: instead of .99, this company ends its prices in .88. The 11-cent difference is not significant when it comes to major purchases like appliances, and it is so uncommon that it grabs consumers' attention - it gives the impression that the items are marked down from a much higher price. Some companies also play with pricing by setting decreasing numbers like $54.21 as opposed to increasing numbers $45.78. The idea is that the consumer will unconsciously see the price as "falling" rather than "rising".

These are just a couple of the many ways you can utilize marketing strategies on your daily operation to help maximize your profits and revenue – do your research and find strategies that'll work best for your business and implement them by including them in your operations manual. Your goal is to maximize the dollar amount each customer spends every time they walk in the door or does business with you.

Operation proclamation:
- You need an operations manual that guides your daily operation
- Have a manual for each position with job description and duties
- Your operations manual should explain in detail the procedures for opening and closing, cash registers, cleaning, accounting / keeping receipts, inventory, security, computer maintenance, employee timekeeping, HR, benefits administration
- Have a randomized time and date for your deposits to avoid being targeted by thieves
- The customer is always right
- Empower your employees so that they don't have to consult a manager to make decisions
- Remember the Platinum Rule
- Remember that not everything is about profit; sometimes your goal should be about bringing in revenue
- Remember economies of scale and the law of diminishing returns to build packages, the decoy effect, "twofers", combos, and the left-digit effect
- Marketing is something you should always be doing – every single day - to maximize revenue and profits

Networking

"If you want to go fast, go alone. If you want to go far, go with others."
                        -African Proverb

A large part of being a successful business owner involves making connections - with other business owners and with influential people that could potentially become business partners, distributors, suppliers, or even customers.

The key to making these connections is being a master at networking and to do that, you just need to do some very simple things. First, you've learned that you should always look your best, no matter what. Especially in the beginning, you're always representing your business. But in addition to dressing your best and being well-groomed and presentable at all times, your behavior needs to be top-notch at all times. This begins with a couple of things: avoid drinking or drugging if you can and don't ever argue with anyone.

Not drinking or drugging is pretty difficult in this day and age because it is so readily available almost anywhere and anytime; and sometimes friends can tempt us and sometimes even business associates or customers may try to tempt us. But hold strong! Being under the influence of any substance (even certain prescription medications) will change your behavior, and it's usually for the worse. It's the a folly of many people to convince themselves that one drink or one toke won't make a difference, but many observers can tell if you've had one.

Your behavior changes even after one drink; so do your thinking processes, and in this state you put yourself at risk of doing things and making comments that are inconsistent with your normal behavior. Avoid substances and save yourself major setbacks in networking and success in business.

Avoiding arguments with people can be more difficult than avoiding substances and is discussed in more detail in a later chapter. However, it is an important key to networking.

I had a customer walk into my tanning salon once asking questions that led me to believe she didn't understand the point of indoor tanning. I provided all my regular key points to her and she asked why this would be better than just putting on baby oil and going out to her back yard. After explaining the differences in safety, consistency, and reliability, she signed all the forms and tried both a regular tan and a spray tan (a popular combination with regular tanners).

It turned out that this customer was the mother of the most prominent dentist in South Florida – the first to bring the groundbreaking sedation dentistry technique to the tri-county area. She became a regular customer and even told her son about us. Now, he never came to tan and I don't know if he ever referred anyone to our salon but remaining professional – even with a customer who may have a stance against your type of business – may change their mind and may make you some great connections.

In addition to your own attitude and behavior, you can take other proactive actions to boost your network. For example, you can attend business events, trade shows, leader presentations, or even join a networking club.

Business events take place regularly and come in many variations. It could be a single business's grand opening celebration, a ribbon-cutting for a new building or yacht, a marketing party/event, an anniversary celebration, or it could be a gathering of many businesses, like inducting of leaders into some kind of club like a hall of fame, awards celebrations, or fund-raisers/charity events. There are business events going on every day and you can do a web search for your city (or nearest major city) to find listings. There are also major business publications that host events, like Inc.com's Women's Summit (http://women.inc.com), Fortune Conferences (www.fortuneconferences.com),

EntreLeadership Summit (www.EntreLeadership.com/summit), Grant Cardone's 10X Growth Conference (http://10xgrowth.com), and many others.

Trade shows are a gathering of several businesses from around the country or even from around the world at a convention center or similar venue where leaders hold panel discussions, presentations of technological advancements within the industry, presentations with tips on everything from selling to networking, and of course, a main trade floor where several businesses rent booths to display their company's offerings with representatives or owners available to answer questions.

These are great for gathering business cards, but before you attend and try sell everyone you meet, read the chapter on communication and remember to let the other person do all the talking (75/25 Rule). I also list some tips on what to say and do to be memorable later in this chapter.

Leader presentations are events that are held by a business leader or even a motivational speaker. Tim Robbins, Kevin O'Leary, Drew Dudley, and many others regularly present at these on tours throughout the year. You can also find recordings of many of these for free on websites like www.YouTube.com or simply do a web search for "TED Talks" and it will give you hundreds of results to keep you busy.

Networking clubs are perhaps the best way to network with other leaders and rising stars in your community. Many of these clubs have been around for hundreds of years (like the Masons), while others are new. There are many new networking clubs launching every year because they are specific to a new or developing industry (like Artificial Intelligence). But the best clubs are ones that include members from various industries.

Some of the top networking clubs today include BNI, Women in Business Networking, Mastermind groups, Optimists, Kiwanis, and public speaking groups like Toastmasters and The Moth. Most of these require a membership (along with a membership fee) and have other stipulations, like having to attend a certain number of meetings per month, volunteering a certain number of hours per week at a charity, or gathering a specific number of business cards with viable contacts every week. Their membership fees are usually reasonable for an established business, but for a new business it may be a great expense; however, it's very much worth every penny depending on which one you join and what type of business you're in. You can very quickly find these organizations and their requirements with a simple web search.

With ***public speaking groups*** like Toastmasters or the Moth, there's usually a membership and fee requirement that's usually lower than, but their stipulations are generally not as stringent as, networking groups and they allow a lot more time for socializing with other members at meetings and events.

Now, when you're networking, introducing yourself can be a bit intimidating - and most people do this the wrong way. Think about your own interactions at parties, clubs, events, etc. Usually when you meet someone new you trade names and one of you will say, "So what do you do?" And what comes next is about ten minutes of each side reciting their resume and it's all going in one ear and out the other with the other person. Don't be this person!

When giving your name – if it's not a unique name – say it and immediately follow it up with something the other person can use as a mnemonic device. For example, when I introduce myself in a casual way, I'll say, "I'm Gio – like the car. But not Geo Metro; the Geo Storm!" and in a professional environment I'll say, "My name is Crisan – like the delicious breakfast bread but without the 't' because he in America we drink coffee instead."

Cheesy as this may sound, it works. And it works well. The other person will usually try to mirror your introduction in similar manner, but if they don't then you can find a connection between their name and a product or person (one that's not insulting!) and say it to them. Something like, "Oh! Smith, like Granny Smith's delicious cookies!" This serves two purposes: it breaks the ice and it helps both of you remember each other's names.

Next, take the lead with the follow-up question and avoid interview questions like asking what the person does. Instead, try to tell a story. I always have 6 small-talk stories (stories about stuff that truly happened to me) that I tell depending on how I read the person.

Story #1 (Comedy) – When I was a kid there was an ice cream man that drove through our neighborhood every day. One day while we were ordering from him, a second truck passed around us with music playing. Our ice cream man told all the neighborhood kids who had gathered around his truck to step back. He followed her, got out of his car, and asked her to get out so he could teach her a thing or two about stealing his customers.

Then I usually say that I hope to see something exciting like that at the event we're at. Then you can move into interview questions.

Story #2 (Curiosity/Comedy) – I am a twin, so people always ask if we've ever switched places. One time I had to get my driver's license renewed, but I was working three jobs and I had no time for the DMV; I asked my brother to go instead. Little did we know that they would ask me to take a new picture, so I spent an entire year with his picture on my license.

Story #3 (Shock/Brief) – I once picked up two hitchhikers and drove them 40 miles just for the story.

Story #4 (Awe/Fear) – I was vacationing in Colorado with my girlfriend at the time and went skiing. When the lift came around and bumped us from behind, I fell into the seat just fine but my girlfriend landed on the edge of the seat and couldn't scoot back because of her poles. As we rose higher off the ground the chair rocked and she slid forward more and more to where she had to drop her poles and was left hanging for her life. I grabbed her hand and we had to get off at the next drop. She cried the entire way as she scooted back down the slope on her butt.

The other two stories are one that strikes thought or provokes discussion like twins from different fathers or twins born in two different countries; the last one is about a time I was in nursing school and had a psych rotation where we had to take down two patients who became violent. Their brains had been fried by bath salts and they were on experimental drugs for treatment at the facility.

If the other person beats you to it and manages to ask what you do before you can throw in a small-talk story first, mention what you do and tell a funny story that happened with your business – make it memorable so that the next time this person sees you and all 3,000 other people they met that day they will remember that you're the breakfast sandwich that likes to pick up hitchhikers.

When you tell each other what you do, that's the time to exchange business cards. Immediately write down 3-4 personal things about the person on the back of their card; things like if they just had a baby, if they're opening a new store, if they're introducing a new product, if they're having a surgery soon, etc. You will need this information when you contact them the following week to get their personal social media accounts (not their business ones) and when you contact them again *every four months* or so.

When you call them for their social media contacts just do more small talk stories - maybe about something or someone you met that was amusing or funny and then ask for the person's contact information. If they refuse, it's ok. Don't contact them again until four months later; do it more often than that and you *will* lose the contact. Every four months you'll contact them and simply say something like this:

"Hey Smith with the cookies!

It's me: the breakfast sandwich sans the tea. Still fighting off mental patients here at Fluharty and Johnson; I was wondering how you're doing? How'd your foot surgery go?

Anyway, write me back if at least to say hello.

-Crisan"

Short, sweet, and you will make this contact a very close friend even though you'll only write to each other three times per year. What'll happen as a result is they will put you at a higher status than all 3,000 of the other people whose cards they got who are sending them emails every day trying to sell them their products. Do this with all your secondary contacts – set a full day aside to do only these emails and it won't be so bad. Three days a year = lifelong, deep contacts. I guarantee whenever they travel to your area or they have a friend who's going to your area, they'll think of you first and refer their friend straight to you.

This reinforces what you've learned in the sales chapter, that one of the best ways to sell is to try not to try – what the Japanese call *uwe*. This same concept holds true when you're trying to build your network. Although it seems counterintuitive, the best way to build a network is to not try. Instead, you should make yourself valuable by providing information or becoming a source of knowledge that others seek out.

Keep this in mind when contacting the people you've gathered business cards from; do not harass people with sales pitches because that will close your connection very quickly. A simple hello is fine unless they seek you out; make yourself scarce and people will seek you out even more.

Also, don't be afraid to say no; and if you ever need to say no to somebody, don't give an excuse. For example, if a prospective supplier invites you to take a tour of their warehouse but you simply can't do it, don't say, "I'm sorry, I have a commitment that week." The person inviting you will have a rebuttal immediately at hand and you will then be stuck having to do it. Every time you give an excuse, you're basically telegraphing that you do wanna do it, and if things were slightly different, you would do it.

However, if you simply say, "I'm sorry, I can't do it," there can be no rebuttal. If the person asks why, just say, "I'm over-committed. Perhaps sometime in the near future – but thanks for the invitation."

Building a network:
- As a business owner, you need to build a network of business partners that can help you build your brand
- Try not to try – it's the easiest way to build your network
- Attend industry events, socials, fundraisers, trade shows, and leader presentations – and make connections
- Or join a networking group or public speaking club like Toastmasters or The Moth
- Gather business cards and write a short summary on the back about the person – then contact them every 4 months or so even if just to say hello
- If you need to turn down an invitation, simply say "no" – don't give excuses because they can be rebutted

Opinions and Business

"Don't let the noise of others' opinions drown out your inner voice."
                                        -Steve Jobs

Opinions are very often confused with values. But there are big differences; you can have opinions about values but not values about opinions. Opinions are how a person feels about something, and it doesn't necessarily need to be based in fact; while values are deep held beliefs based on facts, religious beliefs, tradition, or culture. Opinions are usually fleeting, while values are usually held for a long time – even for life.

Having a list of values for your business is a necessity as we discussed in the "values" chapter of this book; opinions, though, have no place in it. If your opinions as a business become public, you will lose customers. If you make opinions part of your values, there will be customers that you will automatically repel.

Take, for example, Starbucks Coffee. Based in Seattle, WA – a very liberal state – the company made its values and opinions very clear from the outset: they were a left-leaning company.

Because of this, they received no blowback when they implemented a no smoking policy on their premises (even outside) at all Starbucks locations nationwide. Their customer base tends to be in favor of regulation and this type of policy.

But it came as no surprise that, when a pair of black men entered a Starbucks in downtown Philadelphia and were arrested after they refused to leave when asked to for not making a purchase, there was a wave of protests that caused the company to close for almost a full day to train all its employees across America on sensitivity.

James John Liautaud, the owner of sandwich chain Jimmy John's Gourmet Sandwiches, caused boycotts of his company in 2011 and 2015 after photos surfaced of him hunting big game animals, including some endangered and threatened species like leopards and African elephants. Even if it was no longer his company (although it is), the company would still suffer from his actions because it bears his name. This is something that continues to resurface intermittently every few years, and probably will for many years to come.

In another example, the founders of Chick-Fil-A have made their positions clear on gay marriage: they have traditional family values and their operating hours reflect the founders' religious views by having a "closed on Sundays" policy. Because they've made some of their opinions part of their company values, the owners' beliefs about gay marriage (they are against it) has not cost them any customers; in fact, they're still the fastest growing fast-food restaurant in the world.

I would be remiss if I didn't mention a major case that even reached the Supreme Court recently. It involves a bakery called Masterpiece Cakeshop owned by Jack Phillips, who is a very religious person and holds religious conservative values. Being a very small business, his personal values and opinions were also the company's values. So, when a gay couple entered his business to request he bake a cake for their wedding, he refused; it was against his religious beliefs and thus his company values to acknowledge a gay marriage by baking the couple a cake. The couple sued him, and the case went all the way to the highest court.

Dick's Sporting Goods also had a controversy; and because they had a "hands off" policy on their opinions and a very neutral set of values, their stock plummeted by almost 15% when they made their opinion known.

After another school shooting in February 2018, Dick's Sporting Goods made a public statement regarding AR-15 rifles and their policy on the buying age for these weapons. With their new policy, customers now had to be 21 or over to make this kind of purchase. The problem with this was that their customers are generally sports fans, who tend to lean right on the political scale. This kind of policy change and opinion cost them dearly.

ESPN has also began discussing politics in almost every one of their shows. However, their customer base is made up primarily of sports fans who tune in to get away from political commentary and focus on sports games. The struggle with ESPN viewership has cost Disney, ESPN's parent company, to begin trying to figure out why they are losing so many viewers; but the answer is clear – if they keep the politics out, people will tune in again.

Finally, ride-sharing company Uber, owned and operated originally by a teenaged CEO, began sending notifications to members on their devices and email addresses calling for support for social and political issues. The problem, however, was that the company was one of the world's largest employers, but they did not treat their employees as such; 33% of their employees lost money every year. Grandstanding while not serving their own employees cost the company many customers and employees; they eventually had to change CEO, restructure the company, and run a massive media campaign to re-build their image. They are still not at the same level in customers or revenue as before the fall.

So this should be a good lesson for all business owners: no matter how you feel about politics or any other controversial topic, you need to keep those opinions to yourself and allow your business to remain neutral. So, be very careful when making a list of values for your business. Unless you only plan to remain a local small business, you must remember that half of your customers will have an opposing view to yours and you may alienate them for making your opinions known. You will have to decide how big you want your company to become and take it from there.

Now, even if you remain opinion-neutral in your corporate policy, you will have almost daily conversations in which customers, suppliers, or business partners will tell you *their* opinions. Do not judge them for their opinions! If – no, when – it comes up, just tell the person that you don't really follow politics or that you don't discuss controversial subjects.

If the person presses you for your opinion or stance, you must remain strong and simply tell them again, then change the subject. Tell them of an amusing news story you heard or a great book, article, or story you read or a superb movie you watched.

Even if you agree with the person's point of view you have to resist joining in on the discussion. Believe me when I tell you: once you open that door, that person will discuss only that subject whenever they see you. And you won't be alone with that person every time – another customer, supplier, or business partner may overhear and they may not agree with you. So make sure you make your boundaries known and stick to your guns about these kinds of discussions.

You can always quietly agree to disagree.

Your opinions:
- Opinions are different than values and don't belong in your business
- Decide if you want to be a national or international business or to remain a local small business – if you want to grow beyond your city and don't want to alienate half of your customers, keep your opinions to yourself
- Avoid politics
- Don't judge your customers, suppliers, or business partners for their views or opinions

Criticism and Business

"Neither let us be slandered from our duty by false accusations against us, nor frightened from it by menaces of destruction to the government nor of dungeons to ourselves. Let us have faith that right makes might, and in that faith let us to the end dare to do our duty as we understand it."
                                              -Abraham Lincoln

The 2016 presidential election was nothing if not a very contentious one. But something that aspiring politicians and would-be leaders gleaned from the events leading up to the eventual result is that leadership always comes with its share of criticism. And we don't even have to go so far as a presidential election to see where criticism has struck leaders in the business world, as well as the results of the varied responses to said criticisms.

Take, for example, the films *Supersize Me* and *Wal-Mart: The High Cost of Low Price*, which criticize corporate giants McDonald's and Walmart, respectively. Both films were met with media blitzes from the criticized companies blasting the films and the filmmakers themselves for portraying facts inaccurately or for distorting them altogether.

McDonald's responded to *Supersize Me* with advertisements, press releases, and other pushback techniques (such as a social media campaign in which customers could ask the company anything they wanted) in an effort to discredit the filmmaker and the claimed facts as they were portrayed within the film.

In their rush to nip the film's attacks in the proverbial bud, McDonald's, as IGN News's Brian Zoromski points out in an article about the issue, looked to The American Council on Science and Health to certify that these claims made in the film were incorrect. And, as Zoromski points out, although the organization sounds like a legitimate scientific or even governmental group, The American Council on Science and Health had received previous financial backing from companies like Hershey's and Burger King. The organization's stances on most risky health behaviors related to food were beyond questionable.

Wal-Mart took a slightly different approach in its defense strategy: there was a film produced at the same time as *Wal-Mart: The High Cost of Low Price* titled, *Wal-Mart Works: And Why That Makes People C-R-A-Z-Y* that painted the corporate giant in a very positive light – and Wal-Mart promoted it wholeheartedly. The problem, as reported by USA Today's Jim Hopkins, was that the film's post-production delays put it slightly behind its competing documentary in its release schedule. This allowed the critical film to succeed with audiences worldwide, while the second, more positive film became dust in the wind.

These two companies reacted in a very similar way that our top presidential candidates did in 2018 every time a new attack ad or factoid was leaked to the media. Sure, it's wise words from Commodore Perry that tell us to not give up the ship, but one needs to first assess what it is they're defending before making such a commitment.

Let's say, in keeping with Commodore Perry's field of expertise, that you are the captain of a ship. So, in the first scenario you are the captain of a cruise ship, and a band of pirates comes to sink your ship so that they can take the women and money. Your philosophy to fight to the death defending the ship and its contents then becomes your duty, as it is so eloquently described by Abraham Lincoln in the quote at the beginning of this chapter.

Scenario two, however, has you commandeering a ship loaded with explosives. These sticks of dynamite are to be used to help sink an island off the coast of Australia. A band of Greenpeace protesters sails up with flaming arrows, ready to set your ship ablaze. They tell you what the sinking of this island could mean to the people of Australia, and also to the millions of marine creatures who dwell in the coral reefs below. In most instances, I would hope your choice here would be to help the men and women of Greenpeace to sink your ship, rather than try to defend a ship full of dangerous explosives meant to sink an island.

The difference here is not a question of duty, but rather the value of the contents of your ship; and by value I mean the value to your crew, your customers, and to the world at large. Also up for consideration is the motive of the pirates you encountered, and whether they represent the ideal in the minds of the many, as opposed to the minds of the very few.

To clarify this further, I'll take you back to McDonald's and Walmart. McDonald's knew that they were serving food that was unhealthy and their customers knew it, too. Anybody who claims they didn't know that fast food is generally unhealthy is lying or has been living in that coral reef in Australia for too long. But, rather than simply tell the world that yes, their food is unhealthy and the film has given them a new mission – to create a "healthy alternatives" menu – they chose to fight with flaming swords on the deck of their dynamite-filled ship. It was a losing battle, even if they won it!

Had McDonald's used the tactic I described in the first fictitious scenario, which is to acknowledge their wrongdoing and claiming it to be a motivator to do better, they would have turned some very negative publicity into very positive publicity - and all for free. People would likely have poured in and reinvigorated their sales because of their curiosity to try the new healthy menu options.

Then we have Walmart, who did something similar to McDonald's in trying to highlight the positive aspects of their business with an opposing film. They could have done themselves and that film a favor by acknowledging their shortcomings and committing to doing those things that were criticized better, all the while promoting the good things they do for the communities in which they do business - like creating jobs and providing low costs on everyday essentials like groceries and clothing; but they didn't.

Both companies eventually had to make the changes and then actively promote those changes as I described above, but their reluctance to accept the criticism and admit their shortcomings right away cost them. They could have had free publicity in promoting their changes.

* * *

Understand also that criticism doesn't always come in the form of a film documentary or some major public announcement. There are times when you'll have an individual or a competitor (big or small) say something negative about your organization – or maybe even about you personally. Steve Jobs once famously said, "Don't let the noise of others' opinions drown out your inner voice." Remember that criticisms are just that: *noise*; if you can tune it out or avoid seeing any harsh, unproductive criticism, then do so!

Responding to social media website comments or small public criticisms is always a bad idea. People will share your comments, maybe even take things out of context, and it all may go viral or worse: it may make the news. Plus, it makes you look petty and reflects *very poorly* on your business.

Following are a few guidelines for when your business receives some negative feedback.

1. The way of the Stoics is often misunderstood by people because they assume that the Stoics' philosophy was to remain emotionless through both positive and negative experiences. However, this is not true; stoicism as practiced by the Stoics involved embracing emotions, good and bad, but remaining calm and outwardly emotionless when an obstacle or bad experience presented itself.

I recommend you practice stoicism in this way to help you when obstacles arise. It's amazing how remaining stoic in the face of disaster actually helps your mind immediately work on solutions rather than wallowing in the negativity of the situation.

2. Practice meditation daily. Begin your day with meditation and then some sort of physical activity. You won't believe what 10 minutes of meditation and 15 minutes of exercise at the beginning of your day can do for your ability to handle negative situations throughout the day.

3. Avoid constantly being on social media. A good habit to have is to log on to social media early in the morning exclusively to *read* posts from others and then once more at day's end to post your own or to *post replies*. You'll be surprised at how much this will help you avoid snapping back at internet trolls and people with negative intentions for you and your business.

Handling criticism:
- Accept negative criticism as an attempt by the criticizer to help your business improve
- Avoid attacking the accuser
- Ignore social media comments or small public critiques
- Stoicism in the face of criticism helps your business look professional
- Begin every morning with brief meditation and exercise; it does wonders for your attitude the entire day
- Get on social media only twice per day: in the morning to read and in the evening to post and reply

Being a Champion

"A champion is afraid of losing. Everyone else is afraid of winning."
                    -Billie Jean King

This chapter is also going to be a little different than the others. It will be about making yourself into the best version of you by giving you some of my gleanings from books, articles, podcasts, videos, primary sources, and personal experiences in the business world. I have lost most of the attributions, but all of these have helped me in many ways at some point in my life. I hope they also help you.

First, I want to drill the point home that it is imperative that you put the time in to gain success. Running a business - it's not going to be easy… ever. But if you put in the time and show up, your customers will see your passion and commitment and they will respond to that; your employees will as well. Everyone who does business with you will respond positively to that.

But that's the key; you have to *show up*. You have to be early every day and stay late every day. You may have to work seven days a week, through holidays, and you may have to pass on vacations and family events. You may have to sacrifice hobbies and other things you like to do. But it'll all be worth it in the end.

Following is the list of mantras I have built so far (with explanations in parentheses for those that need it); I read all of these every day after my walk, before I shower. I also pick one to focus on every week. This means that I write it on a chit of paper and read it every couple of hours every day for that week and try to follow its message. This may not work for you, but it may still be worth a shot – you never know. I recommend you read them and write down the ones that you think will work for you and during your journey add any new ones you encounter. And every once in a while, write them all down again. Writing them out helps in many more ways than just reading them every day.

*If you can finish a task within 5 minutes, do it now

*For real change to take place, you can't just change what you *do*; you must change what you *believe*

*Find your path

*Be an adult, not a child

*Identify and defy your invisible script (this is from Ramit Sethi. It means that we all have stereotypes that we fall into because of one aspect of our lives. For example, if you have a criminal record, people will stereotype you as always looking for an easy score or as someone who is uneducated and unsuccessful. Or a successful woman is always mean and an authoritarian. The idea is to find what is typically attributed to your "invisible scripts" and make every effort not to fall into them.)

*If you are being interviewed (includes meeting with investors or lenders) then you must reframe it so that you are interviewing *them*

*Treat everything you do like it's a job (includes hobbies, relationships, etc.)

*Embrace boredom (this concept is used by many successful people. It basically means that you need to take time out and let yourself get bored; your mind will begin to wander and form new ideas that it would not normally with all of our daily distractions like technology)

*Have a vision (for your life and your future)

*Make your bed every morning (this one is from Navy SEAL Admiral William H. McCraven. He posits that making your bed every day helps you start your day in order and changes your mentality in ways that you can't imagine.)

*Have a plan (not just a business plan. Just like you must plan for every possible scenario for your business, you should try to have an action plan for unexpected things that may present themselves in your life)

*Make no excuses – you have arms and legs (look up Nick Vujicic online)

*Create a weekly challenge (these can be simple things like do the dishes every night for a week or finish designing the logo for your company by Saturday)

*Take care of the grandpa/grandma in you (this concept is to treat yourself with respect as if you were a grandparent. Don't do things you wouldn't let your grandparent do. So, take your meds, brush your teeth twice per day, etc.)

*Imagine their lives without you (similar to the last one, this is to help you take care of yourself and love yourself, but for this is for the sake of your loved ones)

*You are what you do on a regular basis (for example, if someone asks me "what do you do?" I will tell them I am creative and I love to learn trivia. Then I tell them what I do professionally)

*Follow the hero's journey (look this one up. This concept aims to have you follow the 12 steps of the hero's journey for major events in your life – like starting a business)

*Get in and stay in shape

*Eat right

*You/because (this is a conversational technique to help you avoid speaking too much about yourself. The key is to reframe your conversations to make them about the person you're speaking with. For example,

instead of saying "Wanna come with *me* for some drinks?" you'd say, "Can I join *you* for some drinks?")
*Learn at least 3 small talk stories so you always have something interesting to talk about with people
*Learn at least one clean joke
*Tell everything as a story (for example, instead of telling someone, "When someone flatlines you can't revive them with a defibrillator," tell them, "You know on tv when you see someone flatline at a hospital – what do they usually do? Everyone scrambles shouting things like 'Get a crash cart!' and 'We need to do chest compressions!'; well, did you know that doesn't actually happen? Once you flatline, your heart is dead – a defibrillator is only used to stop your heart from going crazy. It's like those old tv's when they got all staticky and you had to bang them on the side to fix the image.")
*Take the time to do things right the first time
*Try to find out people's motivations (this will help you sell and become valuable to them if you can help them achieve what they want)

*Match your words to the person you're speaking to (so if you're speaking to someone who is not very educated, don't talk about "preponderance of the evidence" – but if you were talking to a judge, then don't say "I ain't done it, yo.")

*The Goose and the Golden Egg (this is a biblical story in which a man has a goose that lays golden eggs and one day he kills it – leaving him without fortune. This is another way of saying, "don't bite the hand that feeds you" but in a slightly different context)

*Aesop's Fable of the Farmer and the Serpent (the gist of this biblical story is that a lady farmer finds a wounded serpent and nurses it back to health. When the serpent bites the farmer, the farmer asks, "Why did you bite me?" to which the serpent replies, "Because I'm a snake." The moral of the story is to always be on guard because most times the stripes on a tiger don't wash away)

*Inspire others

*Win an argument by not being in one (this is from Gerry Spence in *How to Argue and Win Every Time*)

*Find a purpose outside of yourself and dedicate time to it
*Get out of your comfort zone
*Success is only rented - and rent is due daily (this is credited to Rory Vaden)
*The easy way will make your future more difficult – procrastination and instant gratification are like credit cards; the interest will kill you in the future
*Changes aren't permanent – but change is (this is from Neil Peart of the band Rush)
*Don't recruit people – you'll only annoy them (think of the person wo's always trying to get you to join their pyramid scheme or who only talks about that – not fun)
*Don't try to convince anyone of anything (you have your opinions, they have theirs. Simply agree to disagree and leave it at that)
**Always* tell the truth
*Try not to try – *uwe* (this was discussed in other parts of this book)
*Like sharks, those who keep moving will never die
*Don't get rooted out of fear; go on the journey – take the risk

*Try to have only positive goals (example: instead of "don't ever lie" try to make it "always tell the truth")

*Think backwards from your goal to get the steps to your solution (this comes from Chess Master Maurice Ashley. I recommend you look up a video to understand this better)

*Take a tech sabbath (take one day of the week to do things without most of your electronic devices. Walk instead of drive your car, turn off your mobile device for a full day, etc.)

*Take 5 minutes to wallow in positive experiences every day (just stop, close your eyes, and enjoy the moment)

*Never try to hard-sell somebody – your personality is your sales pitch

*Go outside for at least one hour every day

*To be happy you must do several meaningful things on a daily basis

*Have a yearly mastery goal (learn Japanese, learn to draw the human figure, learn computers, etc.)

*The 10-minute rule (practice something for just 10 minutes per day and in just a few months you'll have thousands of hours of practice under your belt)

*Try to do something that terrifies you every single day (approach strangers, ride an elevator to the 30th floor, etc)

*Help someone/make someone's day daily (could be as simple as paying someone a compliment)

*Take a cold shower at least once per week

*Learn to say "no" when you don't want to do something

*Do something or go somewhere new every week

*Be in control; avoid coffee, drugs, liquor, cigarettes

*Get your finances in order

*"There's always a way… when you're committed." (this is from Romacio Fulcher)

*Create an affirmation and repeat it daily

**Every* decision affects who you become

*Avoid living in the rearview; keep looking ahead

*Eat that frog (this is from Mark Twain. He said that if you have a long list of tasks, you should tackle the biggest, hardest one first)

*"Integrity grants you uncontested leadership" (this is from John C. Maxwell)
*My one word (this is from Mike Ashcraft and Rachel Olsen. The concept is to pick one word and live by it for an entire year. Examples that I've used are Execution (of plans) and Focus (on things that matter))
*Leadership has less to do with position than it does disposition (also from John C. Maxwell)
*Associate with right-thinking people (also from John C. Maxwell)
*Never allow others to think you have all the answers; it will make them dependent on you
*Say something uplifting within 60 seconds of every conversation
*Break tasks down into small manageable parts (like reading this 350-page book one 10-page chapter per day)
*Be gracious
*Live mindfully (mindful living is related to meditation. Look this one up for some great articles and videos)
*Boundaries don't limit you; they set you free

*Value your time (as a professional, don't give away your work; if you're a musician, charge for your music; if you're a writer, don't give away your works)
*There is no sure path to success, but one sure path to failure: trying to please everyone (this is from Tim Ferriss)
*If you have a problem, write it down and then throw that piece of paper away (this is a technique one of our presidents used. I think it was Dwight Eisenhower)
*Don't let "potential" be written on your tombstone
*Don't let a higher power be your "Giving Tree"; take responsibility of your life and hold *yourself* accountable
*Silence is powerful
*Focus on breathing to concentrate and find answers (this also comes from meditation)
*Don't say, "I can't"; say, "I don't" (instead of "I can't drink," which will bring about questions of why, etc., say "I don't drink" – and you will have no pushback)
*Follow the Goldilocks Rule (people perform their best when they are assigned to tasks that are not too easy nor too difficult for them, but just slightly above easy and slightly below difficult)

*Discomfort is temporary

*You'll never regret good work once it's done

*If you set your bar at "amazing" it's very difficult to get motivated to even start the task

    *   *   *

Here is a list of books I recommend:

The Miracle Morning by Hal Elrod

How to Argue and Win Every Time by Gerry Spence

The 7 Habits of Highly Effective People by Stephen R. Covey

The 8th Habit by Stephen R. Covey

Think and Grow Rich by Napoleon Hill

The Secret by Rhonda Byrne

Taming Your Gremlin by Rick Carson

Feel the Fear and Do it Anyway y Dr. Susan Jeffers

Meditations by Marcus Aurelius

Creating Competitive Advantage by Jaynie L. Smith

How to Win Friends and Influence People by Dale Carnegie

Make Your Bed by William H. McCraven

The Obstacle is the Way by Ryan Holiday
Life Without Limits by Nick Vujicic
Evolved Enterprise by Yanik Silver
Opportunity by Eben Pagan
WTF?! (Willing to Fail) by Brian Scudamore
Developing the Leader in You by John C. Maxwell
Meditation by Marcus Aurelius
The Art of War by Sun Tzu

If you do your best every day, set a great example, and keep positive even in the face of adversity, you will eventually succeed; and what Joey LaMotta says on *Raging Bull* will become true: "If you win, you win; if you lose, you still win!"

The Folly of Being a Low-Cost Provider

"You buy cheaply, you pay dearly."
                    -French Proverb

It is often very tempting when a company finds itself in financial trouble (or perhaps finds itself in the midst of a vicious war against its competitors, all vying for the business of a limited number of customers) to lower prices in an effort to beat out the competition. This chapter will address why this is a big mistake.

There is an old saying (with many variations to fit the industry that uses it) that says that customers have three options when choosing their services: cheap, fast, and good. The customer, however can ever only have two of these at any one time. So, if it's cheap and fast, it's not gonna be good; f it's cheap and good, it's not gonna be fast; and if it's good and fast, it's not gonna be cheap.

Of course, some variations will use "nice" instead of "fast" or whatever, but good and cheap are always two of the components.

The reason this is such a good point to keep in mind when you're in business is that it's true. Just think about it: it's absolutely impossible to have a product that's nice and works perfectly but is also the least expensive on the market. Look at the Apple iPhone; even though they're made in China, these devices are the most expensive on the market because they look very nice and they work very, very well.

If you are a manufacturer who finds himself competing based solely on price, congratulations – you've just become a **commodity**. When thinking of what a commodity is, think of the word *common*. Pencils, paper – well, most office supplies – as well as basic groceries like meats and milk, and kitchen essentials like garbage bags and brooms; these are all commodities because there are 1,000,001 manufacturers of the exact same product, and chances are they're all made in the same factory in China.

Competing on price means you'll have extremely low margins, which in turn means you have to sell a heck of a lot of these items for there to be any kind of sustainability for your business. This also means that you'll need a very large marketing budget just to maintain a large enough customer base to stay afloat.

A low price is a sign of desperation for a company. It means that the company is in such dire straits that they have decided to remove any barriers to entry for competitors – or that the company fears that they're about to become a commodity and have decided that their only advantage will be the low price. But remember that *a low price is not a competitive advantage.*

Payless Shoesource tried to prove this in December 2018 when they secretly opened a shoe store called "Palessi" in a high-end mall. The retailer used their regular products but re-packaged them with fancy-looking boxes and bags and priced their shoes and boots at up to 1,080 times the price they charged at Payless. They were the same shoes, simply repackaged. The influencers Payless invited to the grand opening raved about the quality of the shoes and gladly paid the inflated prices, only to find out at the end of the event that they were actually Payless shoes.

Payless was trying to prove that their inexpensive shoes could pass for expensive ones; what they truly proved was that price and branding has a very big influence on a consumer's perceptions about the product. Remember, a competitive advantage should be something that a competitor can't easily replicate. Even a giant with strong purchasing power like Wal-Mart and McDonald's doesn't always have the lowest price on everything, even if their competitive advantage is primarily the leverage they have with suppliers.

Even worse is if you're a service company that competes on price. Customers want a fair price on services, but they're also wary of "el cheapo"-type businesses.

The lesson here is that a cheap pool service could be interpreted to mean that your pool service person may be a felon on parole who's looking for his next house to rob; a cheap delivery service could mean the delivery people they hire are new drivers who easily get lost or deliver to the wrong place; and a cheap electrician could mean she is self-taught and may cause a short-circuit that burns your entire property down.

Before making the decision to compete on price you need to go back and really think hard about the "cheap, nice, and good" adage. If "cheap" is going to be one of your two services, then it *must* go with either "nice" or "good" – and remember that cheap doesn't necessarily mean "cheapest". In fact, it should *never* mean "cheapest". But once you determine what type of company you're going to be, play up your *other* advantages before you play up your low price.

Being a low-cost provider:
- If you find that the only way you can compete is based on price, then you've become a commodity
- Competing on price means you'll have very low margins
- Low margins means you have to spend more on marketing to build a very large customer base
- A low price is not a barrier to entry for competitors
- Being the lowest-priced usually means you have the lowest-quality product or service
- Having good branding and mid- or high prices can be perceived by consumers as a sign of the quality of the product or service
- Avoid being a low-cost provider unless your competitive advantage is purchasing power or economies of scale

Your Weaknesses

"Nature is as well adapted as to our weakness as to our strength."
                            -Henry David Thoreau

It's easy to think that, once your company is at least somewhat successful, you're doing everything right and there is no need to make any changes. But this is in fact the best time to step back and assess your weaknesses, or at least to try and identify where your opportunities for growth lie.

Weaknesses are important for you to be aware of because this is what competitors will use against you to gain an advantage and steal your customers. We discussed in the "Know Your Numbers" chapter that knowing your numbers is a great way to find out where some of your shortcomings lie; perhaps your costs of manufacturing are too high. There is never a bad time to be on the lookout for reducing your manufacturing costs.

If you are in a service industry, then your costs may be coming in the form of inefficiencies in your process. It's a good habit to spend an entire day every quarter analyzing your processes. When I say an entire day, I mean it – really spend time looking at everything about your process to determine if it is working at its optimum.

Additionally, even if a process is at its most efficient one quarter, it doesn't necessarily mean that the next quarter the same process is effective. Things change: laws change; people change; your customers' wants and needs change; technology changes. There are so many factors that can affect your process or just business in general that you need to always be on top of things as an owner.

It could also be that your prices are too low or too high. Again, it's important to spend an entire day at least every quarter to analyze the market. What are the trends? Are people looking for healthier food options?

Perhaps your menu needs to reflect that. Maybe people are shifting to changing their oil every 5,000 miles (as most car manufacturers recommend in their owner's manuals) instead of every 3,000. Your prices would need to reflect this change in behavior.

Your competition is also a great indicator of where you should be. Competition should be analyzed every week – because they can make changes on a dime that will undercut you and can cost you a ton of money with lost customers, promotions, or even new product offerings. Always keep ahead of your competition; maybe send a secret shopper their way to see how they interact with customers or how their store layout is or how their marketing materials and products are displayed (known as **_merchandising_**).

It is also a good idea to get customer feedback on ways you can improve. We discussed this in the chapter on communication, but it is important for you to really do this on a regular enough basis so that if you begin to falter somewhere, you can fix it before it becomes a *major* problem.

Running reports and analytics for your business can also help you identify if your business is seasonal. If it is, then you'll need to quickly formulate a plan to offset the lower revenues from the off-season.

Every few years you will also need to determine if your logo has become outdated or if socio-political changes in the country have made your logo obsolete. It can happen; look at the Washington Redskins football team: a sudden charge of outrage at the insensitivity of the team's logo and name stirred up a popular call for change. The organization, although it had had a similar logo and the same name for decades, now found itself in the middle of a controversy because of socio-political changes.

Even if it's not caused by a major socio-political demand for change, sometimes logos become dated. Even if it looks today like your logo is timeless, a freshening up of your company image is sometimes enough to stir up customer curiosity or to reinvigorate your sales. This can also be achieved by changing the interior look of your business, with some inexpensive changes to your décor. Customers and employees alike tend to become more motivated when things feel new and different. Plus, it shows you care about your company, your employees, and your customers when you're constantly re-investing in your business.

You'll also want to make sure that, even if you have employees, you work the front lines once in a while to ensure that you are properly staffed. It can't be stressed enough that your business will suffer greatly if you become successful but can't handle the success. This is the ***best-case scenario***.

In a best-case scenario situation, a business has grown too quickly and is unable to handle the growth or the customer demand. You should have planned for this when you made your business plan, but if you didn't, you need to make sure you catch it and do something about it before you start to lose even some of your more loyal customers. You know, the ones who advertise for you for free by word-of-mouth.

Efficiency works both ways, after all. It means utilizing the resources that you have to their fullest, but it also means that you need to have enough resources to take care of things and customers quickly.

This is also true not just for your labor force, but also for your inventory. You shouldn't have so much inventory that it just sits in a warehouse for months before you sell it. Goods, even non-perishable ones, do not fare well if left to sit for long periods of time without use. This is wasteful and costly. However, you should also not have so little inventory that you can't handle customer demand. Find you balance; run reports and analytics to determine sales trends and to be able to streamline your inventory management.

One final note about your weaknesses. Sometimes your weakness is not an internal one, but an external one. It could be that the city you operate in suddenly becomes a ghost town; or perhaps the demographics change, and the new demographic just isn't interested in your product or service. It could also be that one of your suppliers is simply not working out. It happens; some suppliers are better equipped to service small businesses, and if your business grows, you may need to seek out other services that can handle a mid-size or even a large business.

Whatever the case may be, you need to be aware of what's happening not only to your business, but to all the businesses that you in turn do business with.

Regarding your weaknesses:
- When everything seems to be going well it is the best time to assess your weaknesses
- Set calendar reminders for yourself to analyze your process every quarter and make adjustments as necessary
- Also make yourself quarterly reminders to check your pricing structure
- Keep an eye on your competition; shop them every week to see how and what they're doing and compare their merchandising with yours
- Re-invigorate business every few years with a change of logo or layout for your business
- Be mindful of your suppliers and business partners to ensure that they're also working efficiently to service your customers

Kids, Pets, and Your Company

"It is easier to build strong children than to repair broken men."
                              -Frederick Douglass

In early 2017, a North Carolina restaurant called *Caruso's* implemented a "no children under age 5" policy. They were definitely not the first restaurant to do so, but the move came at a time when social media was at its peak. The move drew ire from many patrons and critics, but it also received praise. The media ate it all up.

Parents are very protective of their children, and when they hear of a situation in which another couple's kids have been wronged, they will react as if it had been their own children. Simply hearing a negative story about the treatment of someone else's children can make you lose the business of many families.

However, there are situations in which your primary customer base doesn't feel comfortable if there are crying or noisy children around. *Caruso's* is a high-end restaurant where people go on anniversaries and to propose marriage. Some go there on their first dates.

Your analysis of your key demographic is what should determine whether to be kid-friendly or not – at least if you are in the restaurant or retail business. Safety should be a concern all businesses. But for the most part your company should be not only kid-friendly, it should be kid-enticing.

Fast food restaurants learned this very quickly and began offering small trinkets to children so that in the future they could pester their parents into returning to eat at the establishment. Not long after that, kids' meals were introduced with packaging that was fun and entertaining for the children. Today, McDonald's alone sells close to 100 Happy Meals *per second*.

Hair salons offer lollipops to children; and many gyms offer free daycare so that parents can work out while their kids are entertained by a staff member and numerous toys and activities.

In the south there is a supermarket chain called Publix that offers free cookies to kids whenever they stop by the bakery; plus, there is a loyalty program, so when the child gets his loyalty card punched for the 12th time, his name is entered into a monthly drawing to win a free cookie cake. Needless to say, my son asks me to take him to Publix all the time.

It's not expensive for a business to win over children. All it takes is small, simple trinkets. I wouldn't recommend offering anything edible, simply because it opens you up to certain liabilities if the child has allergies or chokes on a piece of candy; plus, some parents are very finnicky about what their children eat.

Consider having a kids' night where you play games or offer special things for children. If you are a restaurant owner, consider offering a free kids' meal on your slowest night of the week.

But you should without doubt offer something to all kids who come with their parents to your place of business. Learn their names. If the parent ever comes without the child, ask about him or her. Parents love to talk about their kids.

There is also "take your child to work" day. This national holiday offers an opportunity for people to take their children along to shadow them on a typical workday. It's also a great opportunity for you to show your employees that you value them not only as employees, but as people, and that you care about their families.

Many companies do not allow their employees to take their children to their place of work on this day, but it is a disservice to the families and to the children themselves to deny them this opportunity. You never know, your next top performer could be among those children.

There are, of course, certain industries in which it wouldn't be convenient to have children around. For example, a customer service call center may not be appropriate for a bunch of children who may make noise, distract their parents in the middle of a call, or can trip over cables, wires, or just get into trouble. Like with customers, anywhere that a child may be unsafe should be off-limits for employees' children. Most places, though, are ok for kids.

Remember, eventually most people will have children; and when they do, if you do not welcome them with open arms the parents will take their business elsewhere… permanently.

*   *   *

Almost two thirds of U.S. households have at least one pet. Of those, almost all of them consider their pet a member of the family, just like a human. That's why it's extremely important that you consider allowing pets into your place of business.

Many restaurants are getting in on the trend of allowing pets – primarily dogs – at their establishments. Some set a special section where people with pets can sit; others only allow them outside. A few allow them anywhere in the restaurant.

Many retail stores are allowing pets as well, because it's becoming commonplace for people to take their pets with them everywhere. And now with online retail at levels far surpassing brick-and-mortar, people are finding things like pet strollers and pet bags in which they can carry their loved one around a lot easier than before.

Some business owners are concerned about customers who don't like animals or are allergic to them – and this is a seriously valid concern. It's for this reason that I don't recommend full access to animals at your place of business; rather, it would be convenient to fence off a small area where people can place their pets to run around or play while they shop, similar to how many businesses have daycare for children.

Not every business is conducive to animal presence, though. Because of their unpredictable nature, spontaneous urination or defecation, and uncontrolled chewing or shedding, places like grocery stores, certain clothing stores, and some restaurants and bars would not be good for animals to be welcomed. There are exceptions, of course. But if you decide not to allow pets into your place of business, be sure you and your employees are prepared with a consistent and sensible explanation. It could be as simple as, "We have many customers who are allergic" or, "The Health Department doesn't allow it."

There is an online pet supply and food retailer called Chewy.com that allows their employees to take their pets with them to work. The policy makes sense for this company, but it's the next step that has made them so successful so quickly: they send handwritten greeting cards to every single customer every holiday season (they hire card writers and their employees also write cards during down time), they send commissioned paintings of customers' pets who send pictures of their furry children to the company, and they also send flowers to every customer that mentions the passing of a pet.

Close to where I live there is a burger joint called *Burger Stop* that has a "yappy hour" – it's every Wednesday evening, and they provide free doggie burgers and specials on their human burgers, too. The place gets packed and has allowed several people to become regulars for the weekly event – and a small community of dog owners/burger fans has grown.

Think of your own way to celebrate your customers' pets and make a big deal about it. Genuinely embrace people's passion for animals and show that you care, too. It's incredible how loyal customers can be when you show them that you care about their pets.

Customer loyalty is often based on the quality of the product and the customer service. But welcoming customers' and employees' children and pets to your business and treating them as part of your extended family will build relationships unlike any that can be built without; so embrace children and pets – do it in your own special way and watch your business (and community) grow exponentially.

The kids are all right:
- Being kid friendly can help boost your business immensely. Most families make decisions based around their children's needs and likes
- Know your demographic
- Be mindful of safety for children at your business
- Consider allowing children at your business for "take your child to work day"
- 68% of U.S. households have a pet; welcome them, and people will sing your praises
- If you choose not to allow pets, make sure you and your employees are prepared with a sensible explanation that isn't off-putting
- Consider doing special events for pets or kids once per week to help boost business and community

Be Charitable

"You don't have success unless you take someone with you."

-Napoleon Hill

No matter what stage of growth your company is at, you should seriously consider charity an integral part of your business. Charity comes in many forms, from direct monetary donations, inventory donations, giveaways, promotion of a nonprofit organization, collection on behalf of a charitable organization, and volunteering. It can also come in the form of responsible environmental or social operation. The main point, though, is that as a business, you need to balance profitability with social responsibility.

There was an economist named Milton Friedman who was most prominent in the 1970's and 1980's. He was famous for promoting free markets, but infamous for discouraging businesses from making any decisions that didn't directly add to their bottom line. I mentioned at the beginning of this book that your goal in business should be to make money - and that should be your main goal unless you are a not-for-profit organization – but you can be charitable and still make money.

Friedman's statements made him so controversial that people viewed him as greedy and criticized him for promoting irresponsible, greedy business practices. He was so controversial that Gordon Gekko, the slithery character in Oliver Stone's hit 1987 movie *Wall Street*, was loosely based on him.

Those who tell you that there's no such thing as bad publicity don't know anything about business. Although you can't ever please everyone, having such polarizing views or making decisions that make your company seem detached and out for nothing but profits can alienate a very significant percentage of potential customers.

Being charitable makes your company look good in the eyes of the community in which you operate; it telegraphs that you're a human being before you're a greedy business person. Communities like to support businesses they trust and that have a purpose bigger than just making big profits.

People will support your business if they believe in your cause. Being charitable builds trust among community members and even your employees. Business partners can also be affected positively by your message. Plus, as an added benefit, being charitable may have tax benefits. Most charitable donations are tax deductible and can thus reduce your tax liability.

So let's delve deeper into some ways your business can be charitable. The most obvious way to be charitable is to make direct monetary donations. If you are in retail, you'll have people enter your place of business several times per week asking for donations to their cause. Sometimes it's a major organization, sometimes it's a bunch of high school kids looking for donations for an event like a school play. These types of donations are easy for you to track if you pay with a check, but they are the least helpful to *your* business. And although it may initially seem like these are the most helpful to a nonprofit organization, they're not.

Monetary donations are mostly wasted in the form of bureaucracy and administrative costs. Very little actually goes to the cause itself. So, if a charity needs tables for an event they'll be hosting, they'll need about four times the cost of those tables to be able to obtain them when all is said and done.

A better way is through donations of inventory or items. Instead of donating money that'll be wasted in a bureaucratic process, try to donate the tables themselves. If you manufacture tablecloths, maybe donate some of those. Or if you're a florist, donate some flowers. What may seem like very little to you can go a long way to a charity. Plus, most charities will mention your organization in the "thank you" section of their website or during a speech at an event if you donate items to them.

Another way to promote your business and help an organization is through giveaways. With this, you provide some item of (perceived) value so that the charity can auction it or provide it as a prize at an event. Like with donation of inventory, your company will usually be mentioned or even be allowed to have a banner with your company name or logo at their event.

A popular way to help nonprofit organizations is to collect money *on behalf* of the organization. Usually these can be a simple jar that people drop money into or it can be a cutout of a heart, four-leaf clover, Santa hat, or whatever, and people will write their name on it and stick it up on a mural at your business after they make a donation. Sometimes each cutout has the name of a child or a person that the donation symbolically goes to help; the charitable organization then usually sends a representative to collect the donations once a week.

The best way to help a charitable organization actually doesn't cost your company a penny: volunteering. If your company is interested in a cause, you can invite your employees to volunteer their time to help the organization. This could be by working as servers at an event for the charity, or perhaps building a team for a charity walk, or even helping to clean or do inventory for the organization.

In any of these cases, the organization appreciates the free labor, they promote your company via word-of-mouth, and you don't have to spend any money. But make sure you also donate your own time once in a while so that your employees see that you personally care and are willing to get involved.

Finally, sometimes your charitable work is not so well-defined and comes simply as responsible environmental or social operation. Implementing a process that prevents pollution or reduces wastefulness is a way to give back to the community and the world. But your company needs to promote these actions. Don't keep something like this to yourself!

Being socially or environmentally responsible is a big deal and can be a major competitive advantage – so promote it. Make sure your employees mention it to customers, make sure it's on your window display, on your website, social media, business cards, and your marketing.

Just like how celebrities champion a cause and often become the face of certain organizations, your company, too, can become the face of a charitable organization. Pick a cause and make every effort for your company and its employees to be its champions.

Charity and you:
- Balance profitability and social responsibility
- Being charitable not only makes your company look good, but it builds community, loyalty, and may have tax benefits
- Your employees will get motivated if you show passion for a cause
- Being charitable can provide free or inexpensive publicity for your business
- Sharing in your success with others in the community can be a major competitive advantage

Diversify and Defy

"Dream, diversify, and never miss an angle."
-Walt Disney

In the beginning it's important to focus on your core business. But as your company gets bigger, it may become necessary for you to start looking at other ventures that'll help your company grow horizontally.

These ventures could be subsidiaries of your main company, like what Disney did with the expansion into theme parks, or it could be completely different industries like they did with comic books (Marvel) and other entertainment (ABC and ESPN).

These ventures have allowed Disney to remain relevant even as things change in terms of consumer demand for certain industries. Diversification allows a company to use some of their subsidiaries as a buffer when things get bumpy for one of their other companies.

It also opens up the path to great success and profits that wouldn't otherwise be attainable by remaining in a single industry. After all, how much more money could a company make with the same mouse and duck?

General Mills also has separate, horizontal companies that allow it to test other industries without affecting the main brand; for example, they own Darden Restaurants, which owns Olive Garden and used to also own Red Lobster. When Red Lobster struggled financially, Darden sold it to another company.

Another excellent example of horizontal diversification is Amazon.com. The company began as a used book exchange platform. The company slowly began dipping its toes in other ventures, eventually causing some major players in retail (like Toys R' Us) to close their doors for good. The company expanded to many other industries including streaming video, music, and TV, but their current focus is on smart homes (with the purchase of Ring Security) and Artificial Intelligence (with the Amazon Echo).

But these changes were gradual, and the company put a lot of effort and money in promoting each new venture. The danger comes if you diversify too much, though, because then you risk spreading yourself out too thin to remain viable. In these cases, companies have to scale back to reassess their positioning and make an attempt at building back up to their prior glory.

When scaling back, a company should return to what worked well in the beginning – its core business. Generally, this is what the company is well-known for, and the brand can remain a powerful player in its original industry. Growth into the other industries can happen again, but the core company needs to be stable enough to be able to sustain a new subsidiary.

Diversification can also come in the way of a *merger*. In this case, two viable companies "merge" together under a larger umbrella – thus making each of them a subsidiary of the new company. This backwards integration works very well in certain situations, because each brand remains separate and can thus create new subsidiaries themselves.

Mergers between two struggling companies can sometimes help them to rise above the crisis, but it doesn't always work; K-Mart and Sears merged in 2004, but neither company has been able to fully recover from their struggles. The Kmart/Sears merge was actually a purchase by Kmart Holding Company.

A *holding company* is one that "holds" various investments or properties. Holding companies can have varied portfolios of brands, trademarks, and companies, and have decision-making powers at all of the companies they own. Also known as parent companies, these organizations are primarily investment firms that don't really do much other than manage their portfolios. An example of a "backwards" integration of a company into a holding company is Google, Inc., which became a subsidiary of Alphabet, Inc. in 2015. By making the change, Google was now able to focus on its core business while allowing horizontal expansion without affecting the core brand.

Another example – this time not created backwards - is General Motors, which is a holding company for brands like GMC, Cadillac, Chevrolet, Buick, and the now-defunct Pontiac. Like with GM and Pontiac, a holding company can have one brand fail but remain a powerful competitor with its other brands. It's also an example in which brands within the same industry can be held by the same parent company and still be highly successful.

Companies can also diversify through smaller investments; not all of its investments need to be complete companies. For example, a company can invest some of its profits in an investment portfolio similar to those of individual retirement accounts. In this way a company doesn't need to be fully vested in any one company, nor does its upper management need to spend too much time reviewing middle management's decisions, the company's daily operations, or delve too deeply into its financials.

This also allows the holding company to test the waters in certain industries without too much risk. Simply owning a small percentage of a company will allow them to see if the industry is something they'd like to explore further.

Diversification is a necessity in a larger company. Failure to diversify puts your company at risk of failure if suddenly your industry is no longer relevant. But like with anything in business, diversification needs to be a calculated risk, and it needs to be done at the right time.

Diversification:
- At a certain point in your growth, it is important to diversify
- Diversify too much and you could end up spreading yourself too thin, forcing you to scale back
- A holding company is a way for various companies in different industries can focus on their core business while remaining a part of a larger portfolio
- Diversification doesn't have to be done on a large scale. Small investments can be a way to test the waters in a new industry before making a large commitment

Looking Ahead

"Nobody gets to live life backward; that is where your future lies."
                              -Ann Landers

By the end of the 1960's computer mainframes were widely used in corporate America, but they required thousands of man-hours to program using special punch-cards in a complex system of binary inputs and dot-matrix outputs. In the early 1970's, though, Xerox Corporation developed a visual user interface it called PARC, and the Alto personal computer – the first of its kind.

The company utilized the technology internally but only considered making it a commercial or consumer product (in the form of the *Star*) several years later. It was too late, however, as Apple had by this time already developed the Lisa and Macintosh for both commercial and consumer use. Xerox failed to capitalize on what would later become perhaps the single-greatest invention of humankind: the personal computer.

Shelving their PC is a decision Xerox would later publicly regret, because who knows how much different computing would be today had they become the leader in personal computing, rather than IBM and Apple. Instead, Xerox allowed new competitors to enter this new market and to take it over, allowing them to make it in their own image.

This is a lesson in business that can't be stressed enough: if you don't stay on top of the competition by remaining abreast of emerging technologies (or making those new technologies yourself) then you will be left in the dust. Remember that technology changes very quickly, and it can shape your industries in ways you don't expect.

Sometimes you may believe the new technology is simply a fad or that you can wait it out. Minidisc was a technology far superior to CD's, but it was introduced a little too close to the release od CD's; then there were Videodiscs, Laserdiscs, and other technologies that flooded the market before DVD's and Blu-Rays emerged as the winners for digital media. The failed technologies I just listed are used by companies as examples of why sometimes it's good to wait; and although these are not the exception, your company needs to be proactive when new technologies are introduced within your industry.

What this means is that you must be aware of what's out there and you must familiarize yourself with the pros and cons of each. Then ask your customers and your employees what they think of each of the new technologies based on what you've learned and what they themselves have heard. Attend trade shows and discussion panels; ask questions. And then dip your toes in just to test the water. If you can't afford a loss by delving fully into the new technology, test the market instead.

If Blockbuster had done this with kiosks and mail-order rentals, they may still be around today; instead, they gave up the market to RedBox and Netflix. If Waldenbooks had launched a website or e-reader early enough, they might still be around; instead, they allowed Amazon and Barnes and Noble to take over the entire market. And if Airborne Express and DHL had just tested zone pricing for domestic shipments, they may have found themselves in a 4-way competition with UPS and FedEx, rather than ceding the entire market to those two giants.

With that last example you can see that it's not always new technology that can cost your business, but sometimes a change in process or a change in consumer behavior can be the determinant of who the market leader will be. This couldn't be more true than in the fashion industry.

Fashion trends change with the seasons, and sometimes trends fizzle and fade as quickly as they came. In the 1980's, Italian designer Z. Cavaricci created a trouser that was different than anything that had been seen in recent years; it was similar to the trousers of a zoot suit, and at first glance seemed a little silly. But then celebrities began to wear them, and a similar design appeared on one MC Hammer in his hit video "Can't Touch This". Suddenly Z. Cavaricci couldn't keep up with demand.

But, about a year after their great success, Z. Cavaricci pants became a kind of joke, being made fun of in comedy shows and other mediums. The company is still around, as is its signature trouser, but it failed to change with the trends and is now just a sour memory to most people.

Even some iconic brands have to change to remain relevant. Louis Vuitton was famous for decades for its brown and beige LV pattern on leather, but in the early 2000's a new multicolor variant on white leather was introduced to excited consumers. The brand was no longer your mom's brand of purse; it was a modern, attractive product that women and girls of every age wanted to show off.

Fashion is one of the few industries in which consumer behavior changes so rapidly and drives change on a constant basis. However, even food has trends, and your company's future depends on your ability to be able to see these changes coming from miles away. But the only way you'll know whether trends are changing or not is by always keeping an eye on your industry.

*   *   *

Another important reason to diversify is your business may become a ***dependent business***.

Payment processing company PayPal was becoming a big success during the "dot com" explosion, as they allowed secure payment with a credit or debit card to even start-up online retailers; PayPal provided a sense of security and confidence to shoppers who wanted to do business with companies they weren't too familiar with. The company also provided payment for over 70% of purchases from online auction site eBay.com. Most of PayPal's business came from eBay purchases. So it really wasn't a shock when, in 2002, eBay purchased PayPal. PayPal remained the preferred payment method even after eBay branched PayPal back out as its own, independent company. Paypal has since launched several other vertical companies under its umbrella.

Fast forward to now in 2018; eBay has announced that their preferred payment method will no longer be PayPal. It's not yet known how this will affect PayPal, but it's most definitely not going to be good for them.

There's also a product that received a deal on *Shark Tank* recently called "Le Glue". It's basically a glue that's specialized for Lego Building Blocks. It's not always bad to be a dependent company, but keep in mind that no matter what you do, your success will be completely dependent on the success of the other company.

The future:
- You need to constantly look ahead to ensure you stay on top of the competition
- Technology changes quickly – if you miss an opportunity, it could cost you your whole business
- Sometimes it's not technology, but a change in process or in consumer behavior that you need to be aware of
- If you become a dependent company, you may need to create new subsidiaries or sister companies to ensure you don't go out of business if the company you're dependent on goes out of business

When Failure is Your Only Option

"Success is not final, failure is not fatal; it is the courage to continue that counts."
                                    -Winston Churchill

After the failure of the Dreamcast only two years after its release in the U.S., video game giant Sega made the announcement that they would no longer make a bid for share in the video gaming console market. Instead, their focus would be exclusively on arcade games and video games for their prior competitors' consoles, like Xbox and Playstation.

Some observers thought the decision by the Japanese video game giant was premature, given that they were the first in the new wave of advanced consoles and their competition, the Xbox and Playstation 2, were only about a year in the fray. Two years in the life of a gaming console wasn't very long, and they may have had an opportunity to come back.

However, Sega is still around today – 17 years later – and the company doesn't seem to regret its decision. Sometimes a product just isn't right for your company, and that's ok. But you have to be able to detach yourself and take a step back to analyze the situation and really make an objective decision, even if you personally like the product.

There are times when the product is simply ahead of its time. Toiletry manufacturer Unilever introduced a new product for men in the early 1980's. It was a body spray they called "Axis" and advertisements appeared in the pages of GQ and Playboy; but the product simply fell flat. The company shelved the product but didn't outright trash it.

Fast forward to the late 1990's, when the metrosexual movement was moving into high gear. TV shows like *Queer Eye for the Straight Guy* and stores like Express Men became huge hits with a new demographic: men who cared as much about their looks and hygiene as women did.

Unilever capitalized on the chance and re-introduced their body spray product, this time with a shorter name and an appropriately manly marketing campaign. The new "Axe" body spray became such an instant success, the company soon introduced shampoos, deodorants, and body washes.

Many copycat products were introduced shortly after Axe, but none could really capture the appeal that Unilever was able to achieve with its re-launched product.

But there are times when it's not a product or service that isn't working out, but rather the company as a whole. Video rental giant Blockbuster Video was so successful in the 1980's and 1990's that CEO Wayne Huizenga had spun off a music store called Blockbuster Music and was even planning to open a Blockbuster theme park in Florida.

After several missed opportunities, the company simply couldn't catch up with its new competition in the form of RedBox and Netflix, because it failed to capitalize on emerging technologies within its industry.

A very big mistake many companies make when they run into financial trouble is downsizing. Although labor is one of the largest expenses of most companies, it's also an investment that brings in the most return. Human resources is called that because companies understand that their people are important resources or assets.

Circuit City was a major player in consumer electronics and entertainment. Founded in 1949 under the name *Wards Company*, the organization grew nationwide and changed its name to Circuit City in 1984. They enjoyed large successes, peaking at about 200 stores nationwide.

However, in 2008, the company announced it would close 155 stores and lay off most of its workforce in an effort to cut costs and offset losses incurred during the Great Recession. The move didn't do what the company hoped, and in 2009 Circuit City announced it would be closing all its stores for good.

Downsizing your personnel and reducing your marketing budget is like cutting off your nose to spite your face; making such a decision implies that your company believes its shortcomings are with the employees or customers themselves, but this is rarely the case. Compared to the salaries of upper management, front-line employee salaries and benefits are a pittance; the problem is usually something else entirely.

As I've mentioned in several chapters throughout the book, you need to constantly assess where your company's weaknesses truly lie and then quickly correct them. If your company is in such financial dire straits that closure is imminent, laying off employees or stopping all marketing will only make that closure come much quicker.

Think about it: if you no longer advertise, customers will forget about your company and stop shopping there; if you close stores and lay employees off, how are customers supposed to buy your products or do business with you? Now imagine closing 155 stores and think on whether that'll help your company recover or not.

Of course, there are times when things have gotten so bad that there is no other recourse, but then the failure was in your ability to identify this danger sooner. If this is the case, you need to sell all of your assets and close shop as soon as possible. Trying to save a sinking ship will only cause you to eventually sink down with it, and then you'll have nothing left to try again with.

Ronny Shmoel, Circuit City's original founder in 1984, has recently acquired the trademarks and brands and re-launched Circuit City as an online-only retailer. Hopefully this time around he won't make the same mistakes that landed him in that situation in the first place. But one thing you can take away from his example reminds me of John Lennon's famous quote: "Everything will be ok in the end. If it's not ok, it's not the end."

Failure is not the end:
- Sometimes it's necessary for a company to simply allow a product to fail to prevent further losses
- Sometimes a product is not a complete failure; it may just be ahead of its time
- It's a mistake to downsize and cut marketing budgets
- If the writing is on the wall, you may be better off closing the company and selling your assets before they are taken by the financier and before you go bankrupt personally
- You can learn a lot from failure; use a failed opportunity as a chance to grow and find success

When I was in high school my friends and I used to always try to come up with jokes that made you think (we were all big-time nerds). So, when my twin brother Vase and I went fishing one night and I caught a baby hammerhead shark I tried to think of how to tell the story in an interesting way to my friends; and as I was cutting it loose it came to me.

When we got back home and our friends asked how fishing had gone, I told them that I'd caught a headless hammerhead shark. They all looked pretty impressed, until my friend Juan looked up, confused, and said, "Wait - so how'd you know it was a hammerhead?" and everyone broke into laughter.

We invite you to take the time to subscribe to our newsletter at the web address on the next page. We promise not to sell (or give away) your information, and we won't spam you with hundreds of daily emails. You'll only get quality content about once every two to four weeks.

You can also find sample business plans and other business forms that you can use as templates for your own.

And be sure to check out our social media pages which will provide only relevant, quality content at reasonable intervals.

Giovanni Crisan is the author of *Milk, Turkey, and Neurosis: or, How Mother (almost) Ruined My Life* (under the pen name Gracie Ann Feldman) and co-author of the self-help *The Re-Evolution Project* with his brother Vasilie; He's written nine books, as well as numerous articles in publications throughout the world including the American magazine *Unique Me*. He has also owned several businesses, including Tan-go Tanning, Fluharty and Johnson, Papi Inc., and the not-for-profit AAAPE. He currently owns Phase II Publishing, Inc. and lives in Fort Lauderdale, Florida with his family.

Contact Giovanni at:
HeadlessHammerhead@gmail.com
Facebook: www.facebook.com/PhaseIIPublishing
Twitter: @ChrisOhn

Rate this book at:
www.Amazon.com/author/GiovanniCrisan
www.GoodReads.com

www.HeadlessHammerhead.com

www.ingramcontent.com/pod-product-compliance
Lightning Source LLC
Chambersburg PA
CBHW031606210526
45464CB00004B/1453